Praise Him Anyway: The Blessing Is the Storm

Praise Him Anyway:
The Blessing Is the Storm

*Ten Lessons I Learned about God
in Life's Most Challenging Times*

By
STEPHANIE J. BERNARD

RESOURCE *Publications* • Eugene, Oregon

PRAISE HIM ANYWAY: THE BLESSING IS THE STORM
Ten Lessons I Learned about God in Life's Most Challenging Times

Copyright © 2022 Stephanie J. Bernard. All rights reserved. Except for brief quotations in critical publications or reviews, no part of this book may be reproduced in any manner without prior written permission from the publisher. Write: Permissions, Wipf and Stock Publishers, 199 W. 8th Ave., Suite 3, Eugene, OR 97401.

Resource Publications
An Imprint of Wipf and Stock Publishers
199 W. 8th Ave., Suite 3
Eugene, OR 97401

www.wipfandstock.com

PAPERBACK ISBN: 978-1-6667-4367-8
HARDCOVER ISBN: 978-1-6667-4368-5
EBOOK ISBN: 978-1-6667-4369-2

VERSION NUMBER 111622

Scriptures taken from the Holy Bible, New International Version®, NIV®. Copyright © 1973, 1978, 1984, 2011 by Biblica, Inc.™ Used by permission of Zondervan. All rights reserved worldwide. www.zondervan.com The "NIV" and "New International Version" are trademarks registered in the United States Patent and Trademark Office by Biblica, Inc.™

This book is for all the prayer warriors who dried my tears, lifted me up, encouraged me, and guided me as I traveled through my storm; you know who you are. You kept me going when it felt like all was lost. I am forever grateful to you all.

Contents

Preface | IX

LESSON 1
God Wants to Make Your Mountains a Road
The Case of Joseph and Hannah | 1

LESSON 2
Faith Is Nonnegotiable
The Case of Jesus' Disciples and the Woman with the Issue of Blood | 12

LESSON 3
It's Not About You, It's All About God
The Case of Ezekiel and King Saul | 19

LESSON 4
Relying on God Requires Acknowledging Who You Truly Are
The Case of David and Paul | 27

LESSON 5
Control Is an Illusion
The Case of Jonah and Balaam | 33

LESSON 6
Make Sure the Voice You're Heeding Is the Right One
The Case of Peter, Paul, and Judas | 43

LESSON 7
Sometimes the Lord Takes His Time So He Can Get the Most Glory
The Case of Habakkuk and Daniel | 53

LESSON 8
Make Decisions with the Kingdom in Mind
The Case of Hannah and Sarah | 60

LESSON 9
You Can't Choose Which of God's Commands to Follow
The Case of Jesus and the Prodigal Son | 66

LESSON 10
God Does Not Owe You an Explanation
The Case of Job and Paul | 75

Afterword | 83
Bibliography | 87

Preface

If you can surrender to the air, you can ride it.
—Toni Morrison

The year 2020 proved to be, like for many others, a life-changing period for me. A year of revelations and truths coming to the surface—certainties viewed with a clarity that had never been possible before. It was as if we all magically developed 20/20 vision after living in a blurred reality for far too long, as if God was finally lifting the veil from our endlessly shielded eyes. It was a time when my newfound vision led me to question every truth I had ever believed. Is God really good? Is God just? Does it pay to live righteously? I had seen my share of challenges over my forty-plus years, but none came close to the storm now raging in my life. This storm came out of nowhere and threatened to seemingly derail everything I had accomplished thus far, extinguish dreams I had imagined, and destroy hope I'd attained. But God stepped in and let me know he still had plans for me; plans to prosper, not harm me, to give me hope and a future (Jeremiah 29:11). He stepped in to let me know that despite the look of things and the broken pieces in my midst, his grace was and would always be sufficient (2 Corinthians 12:9).

A storm is defined as a fierce disturbance of the normal condition of the atmosphere, evidenced by winds of uncommon force or direction, thunder and lightning, and precipitation, including rain, snow, hail, or sleet. It is a violent assault on the natural order of things, a commotion that jolts you out of the calm you were

Preface

accustomed to, forcing you to reckon with a new state, to renegotiate the way things had been for so long. I recognize now that the calm I had experienced thus far was not a peaceful state that came from relinquishing all my cares to the Lord but instead, a quiet resolve that had given in to the enemy who had been wreaking havoc in my life for more years than I care to admit. I had allowed the pain and disappointments of life to overtake me, swallowing me up to the point that I was non-existent. I was numb. I no longer had the desire or energy to resist or the will to fight off the beast engulfing me. My bitterness, fear, and resentment became the invisible forces taking control, the forces that motivated every move I made. I had given myself over completely to the enemy without even knowing it.

My storm, however, became the rallying cry I needed desperately to get my house in order, the force that made me realize how much I needed to call on the supernatural power, which had always been at my disposal but had often taken a backseat to my limited power. The challenges I had faced throughout my life thus far all appeared to pale in comparison to the obstacles now in my midst, but this storm forced me to evaluate prior experiences, recollect previous difficulties, and remind myself I was still here; God, in his infinite power and wisdom, had carried me through. And more importantly, that same God was still working, even if I could not see or feel him.

I realized this storm, unequivocally, was one I couldn't quell on my own, and that is the power of God at work. He forced me to learn very quickly how much I needed him when I was faced with the reality that I had nothing else. There's nothing like being stripped bare, coming face to face with the awareness that you can do nothing without him, and accepting the reality that no one or anything can appease like God. I had to reassess every assumption I'd ever made, re-envision my identity, and align it and my life course with the will of God. My faith had no choice but to grow if I could just find the strength to surrender—to let go and let God have his way.

LESSON 1

God Wants to Make Your Mountains a Road

The Case of Joseph and Hannah

Navigating Unknown Territory

As a child, I grew up in the historic town of Savannah, Georgia, known for its moss-covered oak trees, azalea-lined streets, and quaint city squares adorned with immaculate homes and quintessential southern charm. The oak trees screamed of hundreds of years of quiet remembrances; vestiges of lives well-lived. I resided in a neighborhood most would equate with the perfect middle-class suburban lifestyle. It was a space comprised of numerous friends and associates, countless folks within a one-mile radius whom I could spend all day with and never grow tired. My days were spent outdoors reveling in all of nature's splendor, which was the only thing needed to keep me occupied; the icing on the cake was that I was near the place on earth where I found the most peace—the ocean. Trips to the beach were my heart's pleasure and could take a seemingly dull day and make it instantly bright. Boredom, I must admit, was not anywhere in my vocabulary back then. Even when my friends were nowhere to be found, I had abundant pursuits to amuse me.

Praise Him Anyway: The Blessing Is the Storm

Besides my close-knit network of friends, I had a mom and dad who loved and protected me, a church family as my foundation, and an extended family I could depend on to make every holiday and blessed event a time to remember. I had roots there that ran deep and gave my life purpose and meaning. I felt I was in heaven or as close to heaven as possible here on earth, but this divine perception was shattered when I heard the words, "We're moving to Atlanta." My heart sank, and I could not completely wrap my head around what that meant, how we could leave the only home I had known and travel to unknown territory. My baby sister had just been born, and I was still adjusting to no longer being an only child, and now this? At ten years old, I was faced with my first true storm. Although it seems small now, I realize every storm has a way of preparing you for the next.

I wish I could say I breezed through this storm with immeasurable grace and accepted the path God was taking me on without hesitation, but the reality is I went kicking and screaming. Although my body moved to Atlanta, my heart and soul remained in Savannah for many years to come. I spent years trying to reconnect with the life I once knew, lamenting my old home and loathing my newfound residence as one inferior in every way to the one I left. I would ask my parents continually, "Why did we have to move here?" I spoke incessantly about how shallow and materialistic folks were in Atlanta and how I missed the down-home, small-town atmosphere that characterized Savannah. I propagated the sentiment that people in Atlanta didn't care about the things in life that really mattered. I honestly don't think I ever entertained the idea that there could possibly be anything positive about Atlanta or anything undesirable about Savannah. I spent so much time mourning my loss that I wasted the time and energy I could have spent making the most of a new adventure. Even though no one could see it outwardly, I harbored regret, which I held onto well into my college years. As the first true storm I encountered in life, I can now admit I fared poorly; I responded to it miserably, but through the struggle, I learned in the end that God has a purpose for every experience he brings our way. I began to recognize that he brought me to Atlanta for a reason, and that fact remained true whether God revealed the reason or not.

    I know now that he brought me through this storm so he could prepare me for many more experiences to come, ones that I could not have endured if I hadn't gone through this one first. So often, we have no idea what God is trying to accomplish, and it feels like he is putting more on us than we can bear, but sometimes, he is preparing us for the blessings he has in store down the line. He is at the wheel steering us in the direction he wills us to go, sustaining us along the way, and providing everything we need. All we need to do is hold on and enjoy the ride. I go back to Savannah now and see folks who never left, never dreamed beyond what was right in front of them, folks that cannot even imagine accomplishing the things in life I have experienced by the grace of God. It became clear that I had to trust that his plans were far better than any I could ever devise. I know now, thirty years later, I would not be where I am today if he had not taken me out of my comfort zone, thrust me into unknown territory to stretch me, expand my horizons, and broaden the field available to me to proclaim his grace and goodness. My faith would not be where it is today if he had kept me in that *perfect* bubble, sheltered from the hardships and challenges of life and protected by all of the resources I had at my disposal. Although we may not see it at the time, victory is in our midst if we allow God to make us uncomfortable for a time to prepare us for the blessings that will surely come if we just trust him.

What the Bible Says

Joseph's Triumphant Ascendance

Genesis 37:3–36 NIV

37 ³ Now Israel loved Joseph more than any of his other sons because he had been born to him in his old age, and he made an ornate robe for him. ⁴ When his brothers saw that

their father loved him more than any of them, they hated him and could not speak a kind word to him.

⁵ Joseph had a dream, and when he told it to his brothers, they hated him all the more. ⁶ He said to them, "Listen to this dream I had: ⁷ We were binding sheaves of grain out in the field when suddenly my sheaf rose and stood upright, while your sheaves gathered around mine and bowed down to it."

⁸ His brothers said to him, "Do you intend to reign over us? Will you actually rule us?" And they hated him all the more because of his dream and what he had said.

⁹ Then he had another dream, and he told it to his brothers. "Listen," he said, "I had another dream, and this time the sun and moon and eleven stars were bowing down to me."

¹⁰ When he told his father as well as his brothers, his father rebuked him and said, "What is this dream you had? Will your mother and I and your brothers actually come and bow down to the ground before you?" ¹¹ His brothers were jealous of him, but his father kept the matter in mind.

¹² Now, his brothers had gone to graze their father's flocks near Shechem, ¹³ and Israel said to Joseph, "As you know, your brothers are grazing the flocks near Shechem. Come, I am going to send you to them."

"Very well," he replied. ¹⁴ So he said to him, "Go and see if all is well with your brothers and with the flocks and bring word back to me." Then he sent him off from the Valley of Hebron.

When Joseph arrived at Shechem, ¹⁵ a man found him wandering around in the fields and asked him, "What are you looking for?"

¹⁶ He replied, "I'm looking for my brothers. Can you tell me where they are grazing their flocks?"

¹⁷ "They have moved on from here," the man answered. "I heard them say, 'Let's go to Dothan.'"

So, Joseph went after his brothers and found them near Dothan. [18] But they saw him in the distance, and before he reached them, they plotted to kill him.

[19] "Here comes that dreamer!" they said to each other. [20] "Come now, let's kill him and throw him into one of these cisterns and say that a ferocious animal devoured him. Then we'll see what comes of his dreams."

[21] When Reuben heard this, he tried to rescue him from their hands. "Let's not take his life," he said. [22] "Don't shed any blood. Throw him into this cistern here in the wilderness, but don't lay a hand on him." Reuben said this to rescue him from them and take him back to his father.

[23] So when Joseph came to his brothers, they stripped him of his robe—the ornate robe he was wearing— [24] and they took him and threw him into the cistern. The cistern was empty; there was no water in it.

[25] As they sat down to eat their meal, they looked up and saw a caravan of Ishmaelites coming from Gilead. Their camels were loaded with spices, balm, and myrrh, and they were on their way to take them down to Egypt.

[26] Judah said to his brothers, "What will we gain if we kill our brother and cover up his blood? [27] Come, let's sell him to the Ishmaelites and not lay our hands on him; after all, he is our brother, our own flesh and blood." His brothers agreed.

[28] So when the Midianite merchants came by, his brothers pulled Joseph up out of the cistern and sold him for twenty shekels of silver to the Ishmaelites, who took him to Egypt.

[29] When Reuben returned to the cistern and saw that Joseph was not there, he tore his clothes. [30] He went back to his brothers and said, "The boy isn't there! Where can I turn now?"

[31] Then they got Joseph's robe, slaughtered a goat, and dipped the robe in the blood. [32] They took the ornate robe back to their

father and said, "We found this. Examine it to see whether it is your son's robe."

³³ He recognized it and said, "It is my son's robe! Some ferocious animal has devoured him. Joseph has surely been torn to pieces."

³⁴ Then Jacob tore his clothes, put on sackcloth, and mourned for his son many days. ³⁵ All his sons and daughters came to comfort him, but he refused to be comforted. "No," he said, "I will continue to mourn until I join my son in the grave." So, his father wept for him.

³⁶ Meanwhile, the Midianites sold Joseph in Egypt to Potiphar, one of Pharaoh's officials, the captain of the guard.

Hannah's Bitter Sacrifice

1 Samuel 1:1–20 NIV

1 There was a certain man from Ramathaim, a Zuphite from the hill country of Ephraim, whose name was Elkanah son of Jeroham, the son of Elihu, the son of Tohu, the son of Zuph, an Ephraimite. ² He had two wives; one was called Hannah and the other Peninnah. Peninnah had children, but Hannah had none.

³ Year after year this man went up from his town to worship and sacrifice to the LORD Almighty at Shiloh, where Hophni and Phinehas, the two sons of Eli, were priests of the LORD. ⁴ Whenever the day came for Elkanah to sacrifice, he would give portions of the meat to his wife Peninnah and to all her sons and daughters. ⁵ But to Hannah he gave a double portion because he loved her, and the LORD had closed her womb. ⁶ Because the LORD had closed Hannah's womb, her rival kept provoking her in order to irritate her. ⁷ This went on year after year. Whenever Hannah went up to the house of the LORD, her rival provoked her till she wept and would not eat. ⁸ Her husband Elkanah would say to her, "Hannah,

why are you weeping? Why don't you eat? Why are you downhearted? Don't I mean more to you than ten sons?"

[9] Once when they had finished eating and drinking in Shiloh, Hannah stood up. Now Eli the priest was sitting on his chair by the doorpost of the LORD's house. [10] In her deep anguish Hannah prayed to the LORD, weeping bitterly. [11] And she made a vow, saying, "LORD Almighty, if you will only look on your servant's misery and remember me, and not forget your servant but give her a son, then I will give him to the LORD for all the days of his life, and no razor will ever be used on his head."

[12] As she kept on praying to the LORD, Eli observed her mouth. [13] Hannah was praying in her heart, and her lips were moving but her voice was not heard. Eli thought she was drunk [14] and said to her, "How long are you going to stay drunk? Put away your wine."

[15] "Not so, my lord," Hannah replied, "I am a woman who is deeply troubled. I have not been drinking wine or beer; I was pouring out my soul to the LORD. [16] Do not take your servant for a wicked woman; I have been praying here out of my great anguish and grief."

[17] Eli answered, "Go in peace, and may the God of Israel grant you what you have asked of him."

[18] She said, "May your servant find favor in your eyes." Then she went her way and ate something, and her face was no longer downcast.

[19] Early the next morning they arose and worshiped before the LORD and then went back to their home at Ramah. Elkanah made love to his wife Hannah, and the LORD remembered her. [20] So in the course of time Hannah became pregnant and gave birth to a son. She named him Samuel, saying, "Because I asked the LORD for him."

Reflecting on God's Word

Isaiah 49:11 speaks of God wanting to make your mountains a road. This is the idea that your obstacles in life can be the pathway to deliverance. It is inconceivable for most of us to comprehend how a challenging experience can lead us to victory, but oftentimes, this path is the only way to our blessing. The mountains the Israelites faced in Isaiah 49 appeared on the surface to hinder the plans of God, but in reality, there's no challenge, difficulty, or problem God cannot use for his purpose. [1]The Israelites had been exiled due to their waywardness and utter disregard for God's will, yet still, God had plans to restore them. They would encounter mountains along the way, but the reality was that God was ultimately in control, allowing the mountains to persist for a time and a reason. God, in his infinite wisdom, will not allow any of our experiences, good or bad, or any of our perceived losses or unexpected turns go to waste. He is indeed working it all together for the good of those who trust him (Romans 8:28). If we grow closer to God in our storms, the healing, transformation, and enlightenment that occurs can be a stepping-stone to bigger and better blessings in Christ Jesus.

This truth is particularly evident in Joseph's life (Genesis 37:1–36, 39–45). Joseph, one of the twelve sons of Jacob, was loved by his father more than any of the other brothers, creating intense jealousy and envy toward him. In fact, his brothers hated him so much that they threw him into a pit and sold him into slavery. However, what his brothers meant for evil, God was able to use for good. Despite everything the brothers attempted to bring him down, the Bible says, "The Lord was with Joseph." (Genesis 39). Everything Joseph did, all that he touched, the Lord made prosperous in his hand. In fact, Joseph became a steward to one of Pharoah's officials, quickly rising up the ranks and then becoming governor of Egypt. His brothers, who once had seeming power over him, would have to bow to him in the end. When a great famine fell upon the nation, Joseph was put in charge of rationing food

---

1. Guzik, Study Guide for Isaiah, §4.

for the citizens. After all his brothers had done, all the harm they inflicted on him, all the pain they brought into his life, and all the disappointment their actions caused, they ultimately had to stand before Joseph pleading their case for sustenance. Their very lives depended on his judgment, mercy, and forgiveness. Oh, how the tables had turned in Joseph's favor, and the beauty of it is Joseph didn't have to do anything except remain faithful to God. Remaining faithful to God was his guiding force throughout his life and culminated in his response to his brothers in the end. Instead of rendering evil for evil, God called him to put on "mercy, kindness, humility, gentleness, and patience" (Colossians 3:12), and that's exactly what he did, leading eventually to reconciliation.

It is a blessing to be in constant communion with the Lord, to put our trust and faith in him alone, for good things are sure to follow. Just as with Joseph, Hannah's story speaks to the importance of remaining faithful through the darkest moments in life. Hannah endured the taunts of her servant Peninnah and others about her inability to conceive, and it grieved her mightily, but she didn't dwell in her anguish, and she didn't take up residence in her indignity. She instead prayed to God in her distress. She turned it all over to him, casting every care on the Lord. He heard her cries and blessed her with Samuel, who would go on to do great work for the Lord, but God did not stop there. When we trust him, God often goes above and beyond. He then blessed her again and again, blessing her with five additional children. Amazing things can happen when we don't allow evil to conquer us but conquer evil by doing good (Romans 12:21).

Isn't it funny how life works and how God can turn things around? In Psalms 110, the Lord says, "Sit at my right hand until I make your enemies a footstool for your feet." Similarly, in 1 Samuel 2:8-9, Hannah offers a prayer of praise to God for "setting the world in order" and "protecting his faithful ones." She knew just as Joseph did that there was no need to resort to vengeance against those who wronged her because God was ultimately in control, and he was more than able to bring about justice in ways far more effective than she ever could. Romans 12:17 says, "Never pay back evil with more evil. Do things in such a way that everyone can see you are honorable. Do all you can to live in peace with everyone." Joseph and Hannah both lived their lives as honorable stewards of God, and it paid off in the end.

Ironically, neither Peninnah nor her children are spoken of ever again in the scriptures, but the impact of Hannah and Samuel's lives on the faith is irrefutable. Because of their faithfulness, the Lord was with them every step of the way, just like he was with Joseph. With all the storms Joseph endured, being betrayed and taken for granted by those closest to him, being lied about and imprisoned, he never once wavered or stopped relying on God, while his brothers were left to come to terms with the guilt of what they did for years to come. The lesson for us all is that if we trust God, and follow his direction, he will never abandon us. He will be with us, carrying us through whatever challenges we face, and these trials can lead to a higher place, a place of prominence, power, and authority. Joseph's brothers were to him what Peninnah was to Hannah, simply mountains on their path to God's favor and immeasurable grace in their lives. Isaiah 41:14–16 says, "you will make chaff of mountains, you will toss them into the air, and the wind will blow them all away." Nothing, not even the tallest mountain, can hinder us when God is on our side. As Elisha said in 2 Kings 6:16, "there are more on our side than theirs"; all we need to do is open our eyes and see it. Our mountains need not impede our progress but can be a conduit to the next best thing in our lives if we are steadfast in our faith and trust in him. Let God take your mountains and make them a pathway to your victory.

Questions to Ponder

- ❂ Can you think of instances in your life when difficult circumstances led to your biggest blessings?
- ❂ How can the experiences of Joseph and Hannah help you see the potential for growth and prosperity in life's storms?

- What are some practical ways you can work to change how you view the storms in your life?
- Meditate on Isaiah 49. What does it tell you about how to navigate life's storms? What are some other good scriptures to meditate on to assist you in this endeavor?

LESSON 2

Faith Is Nonnegotiable
The Case of Jesus' Disciples and the Woman with the Issue of Blood

Questioning My Faith

As I approached my teen years, I started to question everything. I think the teen years, in and of themselves, are a period of numerous storms you endure as you make the trek to adulthood. It comes with the territory—you're trying to figure out where you fit in and how to distinguish your thoughts, ideas, and ways from that of your parents. I was like most teenagers; anything my parents said, I had to counter it. I would question it just for the challenge and to assert my free and independent will. It could have been something mundane, such as not wanting to clean my room, or some more substantive issues.

I remember vividly having a conversation with my mom about faith. I had become disillusioned with the people I engaged with at church and struggled with the contradictions between what I read in the Bible and people's actions. The inconsistencies were so glaring that I questioned the need for the church at all. Everything I had relied on as truth, including my faith, was now up for debate.

My mom patiently attended to my musings. She acknowledged the inconsistencies and the failings of those who professed to be followers of Christ. But she also assured me that the church still served a purpose, even if the folks in it undoubtedly fell short. She made it very clear that the intent and purpose of the church still stand regardless of anyone's actions, and we need to do our part to make it what God intended it to be.

Even today, when I question the actions of Christians, I'm dismayed by the outward rejection of Godly ideals such as love, patience, self-sacrifice, and mercy, or see folks mistreating and devaluing individuals in the name of God, I think back to that conversation. My faith was challenged then and is often challenged still today. It is very easy for us to allow the flaws and inadequacies within us and others to stunt our faith, for such imperfections to act as a stumbling block to truly believing in God's promises. However, I have learned that although true faith will surely be tested, it can withstand such obstacles and is required as we work to embody the purpose of the church.

What the Bible Says

A Woman's Valiant Mission

Luke 8:43–48 NIV

[43] And a woman was there who had been subject to bleeding for twelve years, but no one could heal her. [44] She came up behind him and touched the edge of his cloak, and immediately her bleeding stopped.

[45] "Who touched me?" Jesus asked.

When they all denied it, Peter said, "Master, the people are crowding and pressing against you."

[46] But Jesus said, "Someone touched me; I know that power has gone out from me."

⁴⁷ Then the woman, seeing that she could not go unnoticed, came trembling and fell at his feet. In the presence of all the people, she told why she had touched him and how she had been instantly healed. ⁴⁸ Then he said to her, "Daughter, your faith has healed you. Go in peace."

The Disciples' Shaky Faith

Mark 4:35–40 NIV

³⁵ That day when evening came, he said to his disciples, "Let us go over to the other side." ³⁶ Leaving the crowd behind, they took him along, just as he was, in the boat. There were also other boats with him. ³⁷ A furious squall came up, and the waves broke over the boat so that it was nearly swamped. ³⁸ Jesus was in the stern, sleeping on a cushion. The disciples woke him and said to him, "Teacher, don't you care if we drown?"

³⁹ He got up, rebuked the wind, and said to the waves, "Quiet! Be still!" Then the wind died down and it was completely calm.

⁴⁰ He said to his disciples, "Why are you so afraid? Do you still have no faith?"

Reflecting on God's Word

We've all heard the story of the woman who touched the hem of Jesus' garment and was healed. It speaks to the beauty and wonder that comes from being close to God. There's nothing like being in a storm to either bring you closer to him or draw you further away, depending on your response. This woman understood the magnitude of being in contact with Jesus Christ. She spent twelve years afflicted with a blood disorder and was deemed unclean socially and ceremonially.[1] Touching Jesus was deemed inappropriate at best, so she looked for the most obscure way to make contact, secretly touching the fringe of his cloak. Jesus responded to her

---

1. Guzik, Study Guide for Luke 8, §E2.

immediately, announcing she was healed by her faith. Why did he need to make this fact known to everyone in his midst? Perhaps, he wanted to point out the essential quality of faith so that she and the people around her would not attribute her healing to anything else, or he wanted to show the power of faith so that others watching would be encouraged. Jesus made similar acknowledgments throughout various encounters with individuals in the Bible. In Matthew 9:28–29, he said to two blind men, "Do you believe I can make you see?" and they replied, "Yes, Lord." Then he touched their eyes and noted, "Because of your faith, it will happen."

Hebrews 11:1 states that "faith is the substance of things hoped for, the evidence of things not seen." Often, we think if we're in close proximity to Jesus, that is enough; that our familiarity with him is the end game. But it was not the act of touching Jesus or being close to him that healed these individuals—it was their faith—their belief that Jesus could come through for them in their time of greatest need. It was their complete trust in him to fix whatever issue they were facing. We often miss this critical element. How often do we come in contact with Jesus, but nothing seemingly results from the encounter? We go about our lives in what we call fellowship with God, but nothing about our lives or character reflects his image. Nothing about our lives indicates we have been anywhere in his midst. We go to worship service every week, pray, and study the Bible, but no one from the outside looking in would ever equate our behavior or outlook on life with that of a Christian. We carry the burdens of life on our shoulders, allowing them to weigh us down with despair and hopelessness, not recognizing that Jesus is ready and willing to help us with the load. Perhaps our faith is not where it should be. Perhaps we're praying, but we do not truly embrace the goodness and power of the one we are praying to, and we really do not believe his promises are true even though we profess them daily. Maybe our connection with Jesus has involved empty posturing or has been motivated by bitter obligation and expectations hoisted on us by others, not a genuine love or a sincere interest in accomplishing his will in our lives. Maybe our faith is not really faith at all, merely a mediocre representation, lacking the confidence and conviction that is vital to its true essence.

Unimaginable, unspeakable things can indeed happen when we come to Jesus in faith. But James asserts that "you receive not because you ask not" (James 4:1–3), and even when we do ask, we often ask with the wrong spirit. We must be careful that when we go to Jesus with our requests, we have the right heart, we're asking with the right motivations, and we are confident he is able and willing to answer in his way and his own time. There are numerous stories in the Bible of people who were blessed mightily because of their faith. In Hebrews 11:4–32, we are reminded of these great examples. Abel, who offered a more suitable sacrifice than Cain; Noah, who crafted an ark in expectation of rain, which had never been witnessed before; Abraham, who left home and voyaged to the unfamiliar land that God promised; Moses, who decided to suffer with God's people instead of relish in the pleasures of life with Pharoah; Joshua, who led the people of Israel around the city of Jericho seven times until the walls came tumbling down; and many others. These individuals experienced mighty feats by faith. They "overthrew kingdoms, ruled with justice, and received what God had promised them" (Hebrews 11:33), and these individuals remind us of what true faith can accomplish in our lives today.

The essentiality of faith is further exemplified in Jesus' interactions with his disciples. In Mark 4, Jesus and his disciples were crossing the sea on a mission to save lost souls when Satan attacked them with a mighty windstorm. As many of us do, the disciples panicked, running and pleading to Jesus to save them from the storm. They believed Jesus, sleeping on the boat, had forgotten about them and did not care whether they lived or died. Jesus was not fazed by the storm but utterly shocked by the disciples' lack of faith. In response, he not only rebuked the wind, but he rebuked his disciples.[2] He asked them, "Why are you afraid? Do you *still* have no faith?" (Mark 4:40) After everything the disciples faced with Jesus by their side, they still didn't trust him. How often do we act the same way? That word "still" cannot be overlooked. When

---

2. Smith, Sermon Notes for Mark 4:40, §I.

faced with a storm, we also are quick to forget all the ways God has delivered us before. We forget the power we have at our disposal through a life with Christ, defaulting to a defeatist posture. Why is fear our automatic response? We know through his word that God has not given us a spirit of fear but of power, love, and a sound mind (2 Timothy 1:7). So, why don't we tap into this limitless power? Because the enemy is in our ear, making us question and forget every truth God has ever told us. He plants thoughts in our minds such as, you will fail so why try, you are incompetent, people don't like you, and God doesn't love or care for you. Somehow, we fall prey to irrational thoughts just like the disciples did. We buy into the lies Satan tells us, which insist neither God nor anyone else could love us because of the horrible things we have done, that we can never measure up to what God has called us to be so there's no point in trying, and that the storm we're facing in our lives is insurmountable—there is no clear or possible way out. We start to believe our ship will sink under the pressures of life, but we have forgotten who our captain is.

We forget Jesus Christ is onboard, so our ship is sure to make it through the storm intact.[3] All we must do is hand over the oars, so he can steer the ship and lead us to shore, and we can continue our work for the Lord on the other side. The Bible says that without faith, it is impossible to please him (Hebrews 11:6). It doesn't say it is difficult or challenging to please him, but it is *impossible*. Jesus couldn't make it any clearer in his word how essential faith is to this Christian walk. Yes, the Bible also says, "How good it is to be near God . . ." (Psalms 73:28) but being near him is only part of our mission. It is the difference between believing in God and believing God. Even Satan believes in God, but we are called to something much higher. We are called to believe his word, trust his precepts, and have faith that rests and acts on his promises. We are called to act in ways that showcase this faith and not just profess it with our tongues. Our storms provide us with a unique opportunity to practice our faith. Many say if you want to know what a person is really made of, watch them in a crisis. We have to

3. Henry, Commentary on Mark 4, §8.

remember that during the storms of life, the captain of our ship, Jesus Christ, is on board, so who or what shall we fear? We must put our total faith and trust in him, the only one who can bring us through any storm. This kind of faith will change us and all those around us. In Hebrews 11, we see how faith changed the lives of so many, and these people still speak to us today through their example. Let us continue the call of faith through our lives and the example we, too, leave behind.

Questions to Ponder

- What is typically your initial response when faced with storms in your life?
- How has your faith shown up during these difficult times? Could your faith have been stronger? If so, how?
- How can the experiences of the disciples and the woman with the issue of blood provide you guidance as you endure life's storms?

LESSON 3

It's Not About You, It's All About God

The Case of Ezekiel and King Saul

Questioning God's Goodness

When I was sixteen, the summer before the start of my junior year of high school, I got baptized. I had been thinking about it for years but finally had the guts to follow through. I had long established that God was real and that I wanted him to rule in my life, but this was the step I knew I needed to take to solidify my commitment. After rising from the water, I felt like a new being, like I was now on stable footing, set on a smooth path paved with an army of angels protecting my every step. I felt surely now that God was the captain of my life, he would never allow me to endure immense harm or suffer unbearable pain. Well, I guess I was partly right, but I learned very quickly that this new life was not immune to hardship. Like Satan always does, he was roaming around seeking brand-new prey, and he often attacks us at either our weakest or strongest moments. It was like Satan was just lurking, waiting for me to give my life over to God so that he could swoop in and make me doubt the value of the decision I had just made.

A few weeks after the school year began, one of the biggest storms of my life occurred. On Monday morning, I walked into my first-period human physiology class and was welcomed by empty desks and no teacher. It was just me and one other student trying to make sense of the unusual circumstances. We were both juniors in a class full of seniors, so the news had not made it to our circle yet. Word traveled quickly that Johnnie, one of the students in my class, had committed suicide. The world seemed to stand still, and every thought of a new life in Christ, characterized by rose-colored glasses and pretty rainbows, went out the window. I began to question the very God I had just given my life to. I questioned his love, his justice, and his goodness.

Weeks went by, and I still couldn't understand why a just God would allow such pain, and to be honest, it took many months and the sudden death of another student for me to come to terms with the fact that God's goodness did not depend on my or anyone else's circumstances; he was still good despite them. I learned that the world did not revolve around me or my pain. It was not about me but about God and what he was trying to accomplish in me and those around me. It's a lesson that still resonates today and holds just as much power and veracity as it did thirty years ago.

What the Bible Says

King Saul's Immobilizing Fear

1 Samuel 10:17–24 NIV

[17] Samuel summoned the people of Israel to the LORD at Mizpah [18] and said to them, "This is what the LORD, the God of Israel, says: 'I brought Israel up out of Egypt, and I delivered you from the power of Egypt and all the kingdoms that oppressed you.' [19] But you have now rejected your God, who saves you out of all your disasters and calamities. And you have said, 'No, appoint a king over us.' So now present yourselves before the LORD by your tribes and clans."

²⁰ When Samuel had all Israel come forward by tribes, the tribe of Benjamin was taken by lot. ²¹ Then he brought forward the tribe of Benjamin, clan by clan, and Matri's clan was taken. Finally, Saul, son of Kish was taken. But when they looked for him, he was not to be found. ²² So they inquired further of the LORD, "Has the man come here yet?"

And the LORD said, "Yes, he has hidden himself among the supplies."

²³ They ran and brought him out, and as he stood among the people, he was a head taller than any of the others. ²⁴ Samuel said to all the people, "Do you see the man the LORD has chosen? There is no one like him among all the people."

Then the people shouted, "Long live the king!"

Ezekiel's Valley Experience

Ezekiel 36:17–28 NIV

¹⁷ "Son of man, when the people of Israel were living in their own land, they defiled it by their conduct and their actions. Their conduct was like a woman's monthly uncleanness in my sight. ¹⁸ So I poured out my wrath on them because they had shed blood in the land and because they had defiled it with their idols. ¹⁹ I dispersed them among the nations, and they were scattered through the countries; I judged them according to their conduct and their actions. ²⁰ And wherever they went among the nations they profaned my holy name, for it was said of them, 'These are the LORD's people, and yet they had to leave his land.' ²¹ I had concern for my holy name, which the people of Israel profaned among the nations where they had gone."

²² "Therefore say to the Israelites, 'This is what the Sovereign LORD says: It is not for your sake, people of Israel, that I am going to do these things, but for the sake of my holy name, which you have profaned among the nations where you

have gone. ²³ I will show the holiness of my great name, which has been profaned among the nations, the name you have profaned among them. Then the nations will know that I am the LORD," declares the Sovereign LORD, "when I am proved holy through you before their eyes."

²⁴ "'For I will take you out of the nations; I will gather you from all the countries and bring you back into your own land. ²⁵ I will sprinkle clean water on you, and you will be clean; I will cleanse you from all your impurities and from all your idols. ²⁶ I will give you a new heart and put a new spirit in you; I will remove from you your heart of stone and give you a heart of flesh. ²⁷ And I will put my Spirit in you and move you to follow my decrees and be careful to keep my laws. ²⁸ Then you will live in the land I gave your ancestors; you will be my people, and I will be your God."

Reflecting on God's Word

Perhaps, one of the biggest mistakes we make in our storm is believing that what we are going through is all about us. We quickly take the stance that the world and all its happenings occur with us as the focus and that there couldn't possibly be a context or space we navigate where we are not at the center, where God and others are not concerned with how things will ultimately impact us. I contend that not only do these spaces exist, but they are the most common. The things that occur to us throughout our lives, including our storms, are merely a means of transforming and refining us and those around us into whom God desires us to be. They are not a vehicle for us to become overly consumed and fixated on our concerns and circumstances. Although we as human beings assume the world revolves around us, the reality is that rarely is it about us at all, but it is always about God.

In 1 Samuel 10, Samuel informed the Israelites that Saul was the man God had chosen as their king, stating that "no one in Israel is like him." (1 Samuel 10:24). The Israelites were elated to hear the news that God was granting them their wish for a king, but Saul's response was less assured. As Samuel introduced him to the Israelites, Saul was nowhere to be found. The scriptures note he was hiding behind the baggage in fear. Similarly, when Samuel began to tell Saul he was chosen by God to be king, he responded, "But I'm only from the tribe of Benjamin, the smallest tribe in Israel, and my family is the least important of all the families of that tribe!" (1 Samuel 9:21). Sound familiar? We see a similar scenario when God calls Moses to bring the Israelites out of Egypt. He is quick to bring up his inadequacies, to make excuses for why God's will cannot be actualized through him. And just as in these instances, we, too, are quick to question the calling God has on our lives, either because we are so enamored with sin and its seeming rewards or because we have bought into Satan's lies that we don't have what it takes to accomplish the lofty goals God has planned for us. Just as in Moses' situation, when God was using Saul for his purposes and endeavoring to empower him to do great work, Saul was focused not on God and his great power but himself and his own feebleness.

The saddest part of the story is Samuel had assured Saul that the spirit of the Lord would be on him and that God would be with him as he led as king. He told Saul God would give him everything he needed to be successful in this new role, but Saul never fully believed it. He never completely bought into this truth, and it showed in how he lived out his reign as king. He instead chose to trust in his own understanding, to give more weight to his fears and inadequacies which he could clearly see, versus trusting and having faith in the power and promises of God. During his reign, Saul gave in to his emotions repeatedly, allowing fear, envy, and anger to control him.[1] And in the end, the Lord declared, "I am sorry that I ever made Saul king . . ." (1 Samuel 15:10). Then the spirit of the Lord left Saul, and God replaced it with a "tormenting spirit that filled him with depression and fear." (1 Samuel 16:14). This spirit overtook him, consuming him with anger and jealousy, which drove him to want to take a man's life.

1. Newton, "The Heart of Unrealized Potential," 35–40.

Saul's actions show how dangerous it is to focus more on ourselves than God. How tragic it is to fail to bring our emotions and thoughts captive so that we can focus on God's truths instead of our own fallacies. In Isaiah 41:9, God says, "I have chosen you and will not throw you away; don't be afraid for I am with you. Don't be discouraged for I am your God. I will strengthen you and help you." The truth is Saul was endowed with everything he needed to be a great king, and likewise, God has given us everything we need to accomplish the tasks he has set before us, but so often, we allow ourselves to get in the way. Saul made it about himself instead of God and thus, never became the great king he could have been if he had allowed God to take control.

When we focus on our inadequacies instead of God's greatness, we limit God. We put him in a tiny box, ill-equipped to bring about great happenings in our lives. We make God too small, reducing him to someone lacking the fullness, glory, and power he truly encapsulates. The reality is it is futile to follow a God we don't characterize as mighty. It is hard to justify worshipping and trusting a God we do not believe can overcome our difficulties. And unfortunately, just like Saul, many of us will never become all we could be because we have magnified our insufficiencies and minimized God's proficiencies.

The truth is our inadequacies and weaknesses may be real, but we hold the power of the Holy Spirit within us, and that makes all the difference. Second Corinthians 4:7 shows that God put something of great worth within us, likening us to clay vessels of little value. Why might God put such incredible power within such meager containers? Perhaps, it is to demonstrate to us and everyone in our midst that the great things being accomplished through our lives are by the power of God, not our own.[2] In our storms, especially, we must make sure that we do not lose sight of the power God has placed within us, that we do not get consumed by the weaknesses of the flesh, and that we do not become overrun with self-pity, anger, resentment, guilt, and fear—all things that rob us of being who God wants us to become. God wants nothing

---

2. Guzik, Study Guide for 2 Corinthians 4, §B2.

It's Not About You, It's All About God

but the best for us. We must focus on him, who can supply us with everything we need. We can be used by God if we turn our lives completely over to him and allow him to work wonders. Don't follow Saul's pattern. Remember, it's never about us but always about God.

Ezekiel further showcases this fact as he speaks about the fate of Israel in Ezekiel 37:1, where he compares the Jews' spirituality to a valley of dead bones. The Lord asks if these dead bones can be brought back to life, and Ezekiel responds, "only you know the answer." I, too, can recall many instances in my life where I knew God was able to deliver me from a storm, but I just didn't know if he would. You have moments of doubt where you may question if deliverance is likely or even possible. But the question is not whether God is able to deliver but whether it is his will to do so.

In Ezekiel 36:17–36, God makes it clear that his will ultimately was all that mattered. He showed that preserving his holy name and his mission was paramount, overshadowing all else. The Israelites defamed God's name and character for years by engaging in practices that were shameful and antithetical to his will. Because of this, God exiled them to other nations to teach them a lesson, but their wayward actions in these strange lands threatened to bring even worse damage to God's reputation. The Lord feared other nations would start to question the power and sovereignty of God because of the behavior of his people; that they would question the value of a God who seemingly couldn't save his own people from their sinful state.[3]

I often think about how other people view those of us who profess to be followers of Christ, particularly when we are going through our storms. How do people who do not have a relationship with God view those of us who proclaim to have one? What if our actions bring more shame to God's name than glory? When we're going through our trials, people are watching to see how we will respond. They want to see if the powerful God we say we serve is actually real and if the awesome God we worship can save us from our struggles or at the very least help us through them. We have a

---

3. Smith, Verse by Verse Study on Ezekiel, para 12.

tremendous responsibility to honor and glorify God through our storms, showing the world we truly trust in the God we proclaim.

In Ezekiel, God vowed to restore the people of Israel to their land, not because they deserved it, but because the alternative brought greater dishonor to his name. In Isaiah 43:25, God conveys a similar sentiment when he says he will blot out the Israelites' sins for his own sake. This signifies that at the end of the day, it is always and will forever be about God. He will not allow even the actions of his beloved children to degrade his character. He will go to any lengths necessary to bring glory and honor to his name. Let us do the same, working to ensure our lives are a testament to the goodness, power, and majesty of God. We must ensure that our actions during our storms do not do more damage than good because God is watching, and so is the world. Have you made it more about you, or have you made it all about God?

Questions to Ponder

- ❀ What image of God are you portraying to the world through your response to life's storms? Are you showing the world how to rely on a powerful God to help you through challenging times, or are you focused more on your own limitations and finite strength to handle these situations?

- ❀ Think of a recent storm you went through. What would people around you say your actions reveal about the character of the God you serve?

- ❀ What are some ways you can improve the image you portray to the world about who God is?

LESSON 4

Relying on God Requires Acknowledging Who You Truly Are

The Case of David and Paul

Sudden but Certain Loss

A year and a half into my doctoral program, I decided to take a break to visit my father for his birthday and made plans to stay and spend some time with my family for Easter weekend. I had not been home in a while, and I needed respite from months of studying. I arrived in Tallahassee, Florida, gifts in tow and a heart full of love ready to share, but my weekend getaway suddenly became a two-week stay, and I ended up leaving with a heart forever broken and treasured memories as my newfound gifts.

We celebrated my dad's birthday Thursday, only to be devastated two days later by his sudden passing. Easter morning, at about 1:00 a.m., I received the news that "there was nothing we could do" and "he was gone." I will never forget him leaving the house with my mom hours prior on the way to the emergency room and my last words to him, "Do you want an aspirin?" before he proceeded through the door. I also will never forget getting the call from my mom minutes later urging me to come to the hospital quickly because "they don't have a pulse," and I will never forget breaking down in the emergency room, so distraught that a perfect stranger, noticing our distress, came and prayed over us. During all the chaos, I knew what was happening. My dad suffered from diabetes, high blood pressure, and heart disease for years and struggled mightily to keep them under control. Although I knew all the signs and had feared its approach, I couldn't deny its arrival—the dreaded heart attack and the sudden loss my family and I would have to accept as our new fate.

It was by far one of my weakest moments. I was forced to deal with the loss of a permanent fixture in my life, the patriarch of the family, the one who had always been there. And although the impact the loss caused emotionally and psychologically was evident, the physical ramifications also quickly became clear. The emotional and psychological scars quickly gave way to a lengthy illness that, to this day, even the doctors cannot explain, but I'm sure was brought about by the stress and strain on my body due to the loss. Through it all, it was only by the grace of God, his love, his compassion, and those he sent our way that brought us through. I treasure the memories of church folks visiting us weeks after his death with frequent meals, kind words, and listening ears. I think back on that time now, and I don't think of the pain or the suffering, just the love God allowed to surround us during our time of greatest need. God's loving care, even to this day, overshadowed all else.

When you suffer such a devastating loss, it is hard to negate your fragility and feign strength. Such times leave you in an especially humble state, where you know unequivocally where your power really lies, and you recognize your ubiquitous need for a comforter. During that time, I did everything I could to run to the source of all power and stay connected to it as long as possible. That Easter morning, after learning of my father's passing, I suggested to my mom, "We should go to church." I cried during the whole service, but there was no place then, or still today, I would rather have been than in the presence of the Lord. God did not fail me back then, nor has he ever since.

What the Bible Says

David's Humble Heart

Psalm 23 NIV

The LORD is my shepherd, I lack nothing. ² He makes me lie down in green pastures, he leads me beside quiet waters, ³ he refreshes my soul. He guides me along the right paths for his name's sake. ⁴ Even though I walk through the darkest valley, I will fear no evil, for you are with me; your rod and your staff, they comfort me. ⁵ You prepare a table before me in the presence of my enemies. You anoint my head with oil; my cup overflows.

⁶ Surely your goodness and love will follow me all the days of my life, and I will dwell in the house of the LORD forever.

Paul Delights in Weakness

2 Corinthians 12:6–10 NIV

⁶ Even if I should choose to boast, I would not be a fool, because I would be speaking the truth. But I refrain, so no one will think more of me than is warranted by what I do or say, ⁷ or because of these surpassingly great revelations. Therefore, in order to keep me from becoming conceited, I was given a thorn in my flesh, a messenger of Satan, to torment me. ⁸ Three times I pleaded with the Lord to take it away from me. ⁹ But he said to me, "My grace is sufficient for you, for my power is made perfect in weakness." Therefore, I will boast all the more gladly about my weaknesses, so that Christ's power may rest on me. ¹⁰ That is why, for Christ's sake, I delight in weaknesses, in insults, in hardships, in persecutions, in difficulties. For when I am weak, then I am strong.

Reflecting on God's Word

Depending on God can be very difficult, especially for those of us who believe we have all the answers, have successfully navigated some of life's biggest challenges, and have risen to a level of worldly achievement, seemingly on our own merit. For those of us who have attained several degrees, have moved up in our careers, and whom people come to for advice because we seem to have it all together, it can be almost impossible to acknowledge our very own weaknesses. It may even be a shock to our systems and a bruise to our egos to recognize that we do not know the way out of our storms, and that we need guidance from a higher power.

In Psalm 23, David speaks of the Lord being his shepherd. He pulls from his experience as a shepherd boy, providing continual care and direction for his sheep. He likens the unique relationship between the shepherd and the sheep to our relationship with God. To truly understand this comparison, we must study the characteristics of the sheep juxtaposed with that of the shepherd.

Sheep, by their nature, are hugely dependent on their shepherd. They are apt to wander off from the herd but cannot find their way back or save themselves from harm. Thus, they have no sense of direction or natural way to defend themselves except to run. They are also different from many other mammals in that they cannot nurse their own wounds, and unlike horses or mules, they are not built to carry heavy cargo or burdens because the overwhelming weight would crush them. Some would describe them as thoughtless or gullible and vulnerable to the will of the herd, following the others even if off the side of a cliff to their demise. Thus, they lack discernment and judgment, cannot recognize what is in their best interest and are often content with settling for filth if it satisfies them for the moment, even if something better is right in their midst, just a few steps away. They are also easily frightened and flustered by the slightest threat and stampede easily. But, perhaps the most telling aspect of sheep that is most relevant to us is their inability to right themselves. Sheep are easily cast down or flipped upside down on their backs, and if left in this state too long, they are susceptible to predators and eventual death. They are helpless and in dire straits, if they are not flipped over by the shepherd.[1] And aren't we too like sheep? We get into trouble, a state where we are not in right standing with God, and we need him to come in and put us back on our feet to get us back in the right position with him. Jesus Christ himself paid the ultimate sacrifice to provide us the opportunity to do just that, to stand before God with a clean slate. In our storms, either of our own making or allowed by God for our growth, we desperately need a shepherd to guide and direct us to the point where we are back on track and in proper alignment with his will.

The good thing about sheep is they tend to listen to their leader, which makes it incumbent upon us to make sure we are being led by the right shepherd. Sheep recognize their shepherd's voice and will shun the voice of another that is unfamiliar to them. They recognize the shepherd's voice because they commune with him daily. The shepherd lives with his herd and is everything to it, including its guardian, provider, consoler, and physician. To the shepherd, sheep are valuable assets, and although the shepherd tends to the group as a whole, they treat each individual sheep as if they are special, unique, and worthy of attention. The shepherd shows compassion towards each individually, as evidenced in Luke 15:4–6, where Jesus speaks of going after one sheep that went astray.

The relationship between the sheep and shepherd speaks to the humble heart, those who cannot deny their need for God. Even though many have heard Psalm 23 a million times and may memorize and recite it, those who are self-sufficient and think they can handle things on their own cannot fully grasp the significance of David's prayer. To recognize the need for a shepherd, we first have to acknowledge the sheep in us.[2] We have to admit our faults, recognize our weaknesses, and turn our lives over completely to the will of the shepherd.

---

1. Plagens,"Why Jesus Compares Us to Sheep," para 1–6.
2. Guzik, Study Guide for Psalm 23, §A.

In 2 Corinthians 12:7, after Paul asks for a thorn in his flesh to be taken away, the Lord says to him, "My grace is sufficient, for my power is made perfect in weakness. Therefore, I will boast all the more gladly about my weaknesses, so that Christ's power may rest on me . . ." What if we took a similar posture when we encountered life's many storms and saw them as an opportunity to allow our shepherd to care for us, provide for us, and get us back on the right track? We can use them as an opportunity to grow closer to him, to be the sheep he designed us to be, ones who are in constant communion with the shepherd, following his voice, and remaining obedient and dependent on him to survive. A shepherd is considered one of the lowliest professions, but Jesus took it on for our sake. In John 10:14–15, Jesus says, "I am the good shepherd; I know my own sheep, and they know me, just as my Father knows me and I know the Father. So, I sacrifice my life for the sheep." What a shame for us to take for granted the opportunity to allow him to sustain us, guide us, protect us, and keep us from harm. In our storms, maybe we should proudly profess, "The Lord is my shepherd; I shall not want," and truly mean it.

Questions to Ponder

- What characteristics of the sheep do you most identify with and why?
- How have these characteristics shown themselves during your storms?
- Have you allowed the Lord to really be your shepherd in difficult times? If so, how? If not, what are some practical ways you can surrender to his care in your future storms?
- Meditate on Psalm 23. How can you use this scripture to help you when you're going through your storms?

LESSON 5

Control Is an Illusion
The Case of Jonah and Balaam

Unexpected Turns

In the winter of 2004, I was on the last leg of my journey of educational pursuits. I had successfully finished undergrad and followed it up with two years in a master's program and three years in a doctoral program. I had somewhat seamlessly navigated courses and exams and was now on the cusp of finishing, tackling the much-dreaded dissertation defense. I heard horror stories about people who had completed all their coursework toward a doctoral degree but just could not finish the dissertation. They were called Ph.D. ABD, signifying they had accomplished "all but dissertation." I was sure that would not be me. I can say now that I was, in many ways, naïve, spoiled by the somewhat easy path I'd had thus far. I had become accustomed to not having to face too many bumps along the way, but that was about to change.

I had shared my dissertation proposal with my committee several times and was sure this last step of defending my proposal would just be a formality. It quickly became clear I was mistaken. After presenting my proposed plans to the group, I was bombarded with loads of questions about whether this was the best approach to take, if I had considered the most optimal methods, and if maybe I should just go back to the drawing board and start over. I was forced to witness a team of academics jockeying back and forth for a chance to rip my ideas to shreds to prove to me and everyone else that they were indeed the smartest people in the room. I was completely blindsided, and when I left the room, I was faced with the reality that my three years of planning had been for naught, and I would have to start completely over. For once, I was reckoned with the reality of having absolutely no control. My life, I felt, was in the hands of a group of elite scholars who were bent on making it as hard as possible for me to conquer this last hurdle. My impeccably thought-out plans, including graduating that summer before my nuptials, were quickly thwarted. A storm had come from nowhere, and I had to figure out how to pick up the pieces left behind and make some sense of the damage.

Luckily, I had an advisor who had my back and a God that never fails—what better team to have on your side? God had strategically aligned me with just the right people to help me tackle this seemingly unexpected obstacle. I realize now that this and all other obstacles were never unexpected for God. My advisor and I quickly regrouped, negotiated a few minor changes, made the necessary adjustments, and I successfully defended and finalized my dissertation in time for graduation. There were moments during this storm when I felt it was impossible to overcome this unexpected turn, where my lack of control was unnerving. But I learned then and many instances afterward that control is just an illusion. God's will was going to be done however he saw fit. Not even the greatest, most elite minds in the room could keep God's will from being accomplished. I just had to roll with the punches, stay the course, and trust in the one who had ultimate control to make a way out of no way.

What the Bible Says

Evading God's Call

Jonah 1:1–17 NIV

1 The word of the L ORD came to Jonah, son of Amittai: ² "Go to the great city of Nineveh and preach against it, because its wickedness has come up before me."

³ But Jonah ran away from the L ORD and headed for Tarshish. He went down to Joppa, where he found a ship bound for that port. After paying the fare, he went aboard and sailed for Tarshish to flee from the L ORD.

⁴ Then the L ORD sent a great wind on the sea, and such a violent storm arose that the ship threatened to break up. ⁵ All the sailors were afraid, and each cried out to his own god. And they threw the cargo into the sea to lighten the ship.

But Jonah had gone below deck, where he lay down and fell into a deep sleep. ⁶ The captain went to him and said, "How can you sleep? Get up and call on your god! Maybe he will take notice of us so that we will not perish."

⁷ Then the sailors said to each other, "Come, let us cast lots to find out who is responsible for this calamity." They cast lots and the lot fell on Jonah. ⁸ So they asked him, "Tell us, who is responsible for making all this trouble for us? What kind of work do you do? Where do you come from? What is your country? From what people are you?"

⁹ He answered, "I am a Hebrew and I worship the L ORD, the God of heaven, who made the sea and the dry land."

¹⁰ This terrified them, and they asked, "What have you done?" (They knew he was running away from the L ORD, because he had already told them so.)

¹¹ The sea was getting rougher and rougher. So, they asked him, "What should we do to you to make the sea calm down for us?"

¹² "Pick me up and throw me into the sea," he replied, "and it will become calm. I know that it is my fault that this great storm has come upon you."

¹³ Instead, the men did their best to row back to land. But they could not, for the sea grew even wilder than before. ¹⁴ Then they cried out to the Lord, "Please, Lord, do not let us die for taking this man's life. Do not hold us accountable for killing an innocent man, for you, Lord, have done as you pleased." ¹⁵ Then they took Jonah and threw him overboard, and the raging sea grew calm. ¹⁶ At this the men greatly feared the Lord, and they offered a sacrifice to the Lord and made vows to him.

¹⁷ Now the Lord provided a huge fish to swallow Jonah, and Jonah was in the belly of the fish three days and three nights.

Balaam's Stubborn Defiance

Numbers 22:21-35 NIV

²¹ Balaam got up in the morning, saddled his donkey and went with the Moabite officials. ²² But God was very angry when he went, and the angel of the Lord stood in the road to oppose him. Balaam was riding on his donkey, and his two servants were with him. ²³ When the donkey saw the angel of the Lord standing in the road with a drawn sword in his hand, it turned off the road into a field. Balaam beat it to get it back on the road.

²⁴ Then the angel of the Lord stood in a narrow path through the vineyards, with walls on both sides. ²⁵ When the donkey saw the angel of the Lord, it pressed close to the wall, crushing Balaam's foot against it. So, he beat the donkey again.

²⁶ Then the angel of the Lord moved on ahead and stood in a narrow place where there was no room to turn, either to the right or to the left. ²⁷ When the donkey saw the angel of the Lord, it lay down under Balaam, and he was angry and beat it with his staff. ²⁸ Then the Lord opened the donkey's mouth, and it said to Balaam, "What have I done to you to make you beat me these three times?"

²⁹ Balaam answered the donkey, "You have made a fool of me! If only I had a sword in my hand, I would kill you right now."

³⁰ The donkey said to Balaam, "Am I not your own donkey, which you have always ridden, to this day? Have I been in the habit of doing this to you?"

"No," he said.

³¹ Then the Lord opened Balaam's eyes, and he saw the angel of the Lord standing in the road with his sword drawn. So, he bowed low and fell facedown.

³² The angel of the Lord asked him, "Why have you beaten your donkey these three times? I have come here to oppose you because your path is a reckless one before me. ³³ The donkey saw me and turned away from me these three times. If it had not turned away, I would certainly have killed you by now, but I would have spared it."

³⁴ Balaam said to the angel of the Lord, "I have sinned. I did not realize you were standing in the road to oppose me. Now if you are displeased, I will go back."

³⁵ The angel of the Lord said to Balaam, "Go with the men, but speak only what I tell you." So Balaam went with Balak's officials.

Reflecting on God's Word

At the beginning of my storm, I often wanted to know what was happening, its cause, and, more importantly, how and when God was planning to get me out of it. For many of us, getting out of the storm is our desire more than seeing what God wants to accomplish in the storm or how God can help us grow and mature through life's many challenges. As I journeyed through my trials, it became evident that perhaps my storm would not pass as quickly as I would have liked, so my focus changed, and my attitude shifted. In those moments, understanding God's plans no longer mattered. All I wanted was to see his power at work in my life during my greatest time of need, in whatever way it revealed itself. This gift could be wrapped in the most ornate bows or the most meager trappings—I just needed to see his hand. Some days the hurt and pain were so overwhelming all I could do was cry out, "Help me, Lord," but even still, I relinquished all control, realizing the inescapable truth— I never had any control in the first place.

I envision Jonah having a similar experience after he was thrown overboard following his failed attempt at running from God. God told Jonah to go to Nineveh to preach to its citizens. Like us, he intended to do his own will instead of the Lord's, so he took off headed in the opposite direction, trying to get as far away as possible from the destination God had set for him. But just like us, he very quickly learned the cost of disobedience, the consequence of our stubborn insistence on having our way. Our way can never compare to the plans of God, and as Jonah sat in the belly of a massive fish, I imagine he was forced to come face to face with himself and God. I'm sure he was forced to reckon with the penalties of his flagrant disregard for God's instructions. After several days in the fish, it is possible the fear of whether he would ever be saved from this fate grew to unimaginable depths. He likely wasn't asking, "Why, Lord, have you allowed this to happen?" "What could I have done to prevent this?" "What are you trying to teach me?" No, I'm sure all he cared about was whether God would deliver him from the mess he had created. But, despite wanting deliverance, it did not come immediately for him, and it often does not come quickly for us either.

Although God often chooses not to remove the storm or lessen the burden on our lives, he will provide us moments in the midst of the storm, whispers of God's grace and mercy, showing that he is still at work during our trials. He will provide a gentle nudge saying I'm still here, walking right beside you, encouraging you to keep pushing forward, and holding your hand through the storm. This can display itself in many ways: an unexpected hug from your kids after a long day at work, a "have a blessed day" from your waitress or a call from a friend out of the blue offering to pray with you. God continuously reminds us that he has his army of angels surrounding us, protecting us and lifting us up in our weakest moments. Despite Jonah's disobedience, God never left him. Although it seemed Jonah had fallen into the hands of a vengeful God, he had really been saved by a merciful one. God was with him every step of the way. He provided a great fish to protect him, not destroy him. God saved him from drowning, kept him safe in the belly of the fish, and allowed him to come to his senses and right his wrongs.[1] What a great God we serve!

Much like Jonah, Balaam was a man of many spiritual talents and gifts, but he acted in ways contrary to the will of God. He, too, learned very quickly who was really in control. His love of self and money superseded his desire to please God, ushering him onto a treacherous path, and setting his heart and mind on something he knew was evil. Despite God's warnings, he continued in his wrongdoing; Balaam's clear rejection of God's will set him up for judgment and lay bare the true contents of his heart.

As Balaam traveled with his donkey, God exercised his control through an angel, which stood on his path. Balaam's donkey recognized the angel of the Lord and heeded his direction, but Balaam could not sense his presence. Oftentimes, just as with Balaam, those with extraordinary gifts and talents forget who supplied these treasures, and they start to think of themselves as better than they should. Sometimes, such gifts can easily obstruct our view of God, getting in the way of us seeing him for who he really is in his grandeur, leaving us feeling as if our own plans are better than his. Balaam not only disregarded the Lord's direction, but he abused his donkey for endeavoring to heed God's call. Much in the same

1. Henry, Commentary on Jonah 1, §IV.

way, we often harm those around us with our blatant disobedience. The donkey represented a meek, dutiful follower of God, one that was sensitive to his guidance. Because of her steadfast reverence for God's way, she became a thorn in the side of wayward Balaam and a constant victim of his insolence.[2] Like Balaam, we are also quick to mistreat and demonize those around us who represent the will of God because the truth is, we don't have the gumption to go directly against God himself, so we attack his advocates instead. How often are there people in our lives trying to lead us the way God wants us to go, and we refuse to listen? And we go beyond that; we take them for granted, even abuse them—the very gifts that God has blessed us with to bring us closer to him, for keeping us from traveling down dark paths that will undoubtedly lead to destruction if we are left to our own devices. We see our advocates as the enemy instead of the real ones: Satan and his underlings, who are actively working to pull us further and further away from God. If we're lucky, God will patiently wait for us to come to our senses, just as with Jonah and Balaam. Eventually, God opened Balaam's eyes so he could see more clearly, and he bowed down, recognizing his folly.

In Balaam's ignorance, he believed God was blessing him by giving him the freedom and control to do what he wanted, but he had no idea what God really had in store for him was judgment.[3] Second Thessalonians 2:11–12 speaks of God causing men to be "greatly deceived," believing the lies of Satan because they "refuse to love and accept the truth that would save them." God allows individuals to believe the untruth that they are or can be their own gods. God will allow the defiant to believe the untruth they crave, not because of his love and kindness or generosity but in judgment for rejecting his way. In Romans 1, we see God give some over to the depravity of their hearts and pleasures in unrighteousness.[4] These individuals believe they are in control and are getting away with their disobedience, but in the end, their prideful acts

2. Guzik, Study Guide for Numbers 22, §C1–4.
3. Jamieson et al., Commentary on Numbers 22, §19–20.
4. Guzik, Study Guide for 2 Thessalonians 2, §A5.

of defiance will be the tools God uses to exact punishment. God allows evil and thus has control over it, but the real blessing is he provides relief to those who want to overcome it. Sometimes, God will make us think we're in control for a while, only to unveil the truth in due time that he was and will always be the only one in control.

I pray that we are not like Jonah or Balaam—that we don't allow our selfish desires to outweigh the desire to please God. We must make sure our hearts are not hardened and that God does not give us over to our sinful wishes, allowing us to venture down dangerous paths. I pray we recognize who is really in control before it is everlasting too late. Like many of us, Jonah and Balaam made life far more difficult than it had to be by trying to do things their own way instead of heeding God's call. Even Jesus submitted to the will of God, as evidenced by John 5:30 when he said, "I can do nothing on my own . . . I carry out the will of the one who sent me, not my own will." If Jesus, himself, understood the control God had over his life, shouldn't we take a similar posture?

In our storms, we often do everything we can to fight God working in our situation, intent on not enduring the pain and discomfort of self-reflection, change, and ultimately growth. Balaam and Jonah's stories both end badly, with two bitter men unsatisfied, forever chasing after the matters of their own flesh and heart. If we're lucky, God may be long-suffering with us, affording us the precious gift of time to get things right with him. But we have to be willing to let God take the reins, recognizing that our way will lead us astray every time, and our finite wisdom will take us on a wayward path leading nowhere good. We must remember that our ways are not his ways and acknowledge with all our hearts who is really in control before it is too late.

Questions to Ponder

- ❀ Can you think of instances in your life when you were like Jonah or Balaam and rejected the will of God, choosing to do things your way instead?

- What was the outcome? How do you think the outcome would have differed if you chose God's path instead of your own?
- How can the experiences of Jonah and Balaam help you as you make decisions in life's future storms?

LESSON 6

Make Sure the Voice You're Heeding Is the Right One

The Case of Peter, Paul, and Judas

Conflict in Our Midst

After a year of marriage, a friend asked me how the first year went. I don't recall my response, but the look on my face must have said it all. She replied, "Yeah, that's how I felt after one year too." To say that marriage is hard is indeed the biggest understatement you could make. It often amazes me that people believe marriage will be a bed of roses, and somehow the thorns will miraculously dissolve, and the days will be filled with abounding happiness and minimal conflict. The idea that God could bring two independent beings together, individuals with their own history, unique pasts, and self-determined insights; who had been taught ways of thinking and being that were germane and suitable for their particular context and fuse them together in a glorious union with no struggles, is unrealistic at best. Oh, what a difficult feat, but somehow, we believe our union will be a walk in the park, but we learn quickly what a mangled mess we become if we do not keep God at the center.

I admit I thought I had a pretty realistic view of marriage and that my expectations were sound and reasonable. I had seen the struggles my folks went through, and I felt I knew the pitfalls to avoid. Although I thought I had learned lessons to take into marriage to make it better than what I saw as a child, I failed to realize that those lessons shaped me, my view of family, marriage, and everything. Before I knew it, I found myself recreating and embodying the same patterns I experienced in my childhood, even those I knew were unhealthy or counterproductive.

I saw evidence of the same thing occurring with my husband. I recall conversations we had about the way he communicated with his family. He had come from a family who joked all the time and welcomed friendly bantering as a form of endearment. Whereas I, on the contrary, did not take such teasing lightly, coming from a family that was much more serious, and whose idea of fun involved deep, meaningful conversations about life, faith, and family. For me, the family unit was the core of everything—the nucleus—the best joys came from spending time together and sharing our passions and pursuits. My husband, however, came from a home where the family unit was only the starting point, not necessarily the end, and the family was simply a springboard to numerous other connections that were just as valued. The crazy thing is neither of us was wrong in our belief, but the distinctions made tension absolute. Subsequently, I came to the table wanting him to be my everything, and he was content with me being only part of his story. The differences were glaring, but I'm not sure why we were surprised. They say opposites attract, which is true; it makes for a much more interesting life than butting heads with your twin. I maintain that there's beauty in differences; if we appreciate and value them, they can be a mechanism for strengthening one another. If we're honest, we have to admit there are typically things one partner is naturally good at that the other is not. Our strengths and weaknesses can intermingle, creating a unique opportunity for growth and development. Ultimately, as a unit, we can be a much greater force than we could ever be on our own. But unfortunately, rarely do we embrace the conflict that inevitably arises in any relationship where two whole beings show up in their fullness. We often overlook the truth that conflict is not a possibility—it is a guarantee.

Conflict quickly became a storm in our lives, brewing underneath the surface without us realizing it. Although a natural and expected consequence of any union, conflict can quickly take on a life of its own. For us, we failed to manage the conflict from the beginning, hoping it would somehow go away on its own, but our negligence gave Satan a door in. I see now how Satan moves, how he will magnify your differences and minimize those qualities that drew you together in the first place. The enemy will make you question everything about the relationship that once was so clear. "Are you compatible?" "Is he or she my soul mate?" "Is there someone better out there for me, and I'm missing out?" Satan will plant the seed that "they don't understand me and never will," which, left unmanaged, can blossom into flora you never thought possible. One day "we're too different" becomes "we never should've been together in the first place." But perhaps the real truth is that God brought you two together for a reason. And through his providential wisdom, he has ordained your union and will give you every tool and resource you need to succeed if only you allow him to lead, keep him at the center, and set your will aside, making room for his will to reign. Often, we give Satan our ear instead of God, for it is much more natural to follow the one who substantiates our fears and insecurities than to trust in the promises of God, whose way goes against everything that makes sense to us. Yes, marriage is hard, but I do not believe God created such an incredible institution to leave us in the dark about how to prosper in it. Perhaps one key to success is amplifying God's voice and muffling the enemy's.

What the Bible Says

Paul's Miraculous Transformation

Acts 9:1–15 NIV

9 Meanwhile, Saul was still breathing out murderous threats against the Lord's disciples. He went to the high priest [2] and asked him for letters to the synagogues in Damascus, so that if he found any there who belonged to the Way, whether men or women, he might take them as prisoners to Jerusalem. [3] As he neared Damascus on his journey, suddenly a light from heaven flashed around him. [4] He fell to the ground and heard a voice say to him, "Saul, Saul, why do you persecute me?"

[5] "Who are you, Lord?" Saul asked.

"I am Jesus, whom you are persecuting," he replied. [6] "Now get up and go into the city, and you will be told what you must do."

[7] The men traveling with Saul stood there speechless; they heard the sound but did not see anyone. [8] Saul got up from the ground, but when he opened his eyes, he could see nothing. So, they led him by the hand into Damascus. [9] For three days he was blind and did not eat or drink anything.

[10] In Damascus there was a disciple named Ananias. The Lord called to him in a vision, "Ananias!"

"Yes, Lord," he answered.

[11] The Lord told him, "Go to the house of Judas on Straight Street and ask for a man from Tarsus named Saul, for he is praying. [12] In a vision he has seen a man named Ananias come and place his hands on him to restore his sight."

[13] "Lord," Ananias answered, "I have heard many reports about this man and all the harm he has done to your holy people in Jerusalem. [14] And he has come here with authority from the chief priests to arrest all who call on your name."

¹⁵ But the Lord said to Ananias, "Go! This man is my chosen instrument to proclaim my name to the Gentiles and their kings and the people of Israel."

Judas's Hardened Heart

John 12:1–6 NIV

12 Six days before the Passover, Jesus came to Bethany, where Lazarus lived, whom Jesus had raised from the dead. ² Here a dinner was given in Jesus' honor. Martha served, while Lazarus was among those reclining at the table with him. ³ Then Mary took about a pint of pure nard, an expensive perfume; she poured it on Jesus' feet and wiped his feet with her hair. And the house was filled with the fragrance of the perfume.

⁴ But one of his disciples, Judas Iscariot, who was later to betray him, objected, ⁵ "Why wasn't this perfume sold and the money given to the poor? It was worth a year's wages." ⁶ He did not say this because he cared about the poor but because he was a thief; as keeper of the money bag, he used to help himself to what was put into it.

Peter's Overwhelming Regret

Matt 26:30–35; 57–75 NIV

³⁰ When they had sung a hymn, they went out to the Mount of Olives.

³¹ Then Jesus told them, "This very night you will all fall away on account of me, for it is written:

"'I will strike the shepherd, and the sheep of the flock will be scattered.'

³² But after I have risen, I will go ahead of you into Galilee."

³³ Peter replied, "Even if all fall away on account of you, I never will."

⁳⁴ "Truly I tell you," Jesus answered, "this very night before the rooster crows, you will disown me three times."

³⁵ But Peter declared, "Even if I have to die with you, I will never disown you." And all the other disciples said the same.

⁵⁷ Those who had arrested Jesus took him to Caiaphas the high priest, where the teachers of the law and the elders had assembled. ⁵⁸ But Peter followed him at a distance, right up to the courtyard of the high priest. He entered and sat down with the guards to see the outcome.

⁵⁹ The chief priests and the whole Sanhedrin were looking for false evidence against Jesus so that they could put him to death. ⁶⁰ But they did not find any, though many false witnesses came forward.

Finally, two came forward ⁶¹ and declared, "This fellow said, 'I am able to destroy the temple of God and rebuild it in three days.'"

⁶² Then the high priest stood up and said to Jesus, "Are you not going to answer? What is this testimony that these men are bringing against you?" ⁶³ But Jesus remained silent.

The high priest said to him, "I charge you under oath by the living God: Tell us if you are the Messiah, the Son of God."

⁶⁴ "You have said so," Jesus replied. "But I say to all of you: From now on you will see the Son of Man sitting at the right hand of the Mighty One and coming on the clouds of heaven."

⁶⁵ Then the high priest tore his clothes and said, "He has spoken blasphemy! Why do we need any more witnesses? Look, now you have heard the blasphemy. ⁶⁶ What do you think?"

"He is worthy of death," they answered.

⁶⁷ Then they spit in his face and struck him with their fists. Others slapped him ⁶⁸ and said, "Prophesy to us, Messiah. Who hit you?"

> ⁶⁹ Now Peter was sitting out in the courtyard, and a servant girl came to him. "You also were with Jesus of Galilee," she said.
>
> ⁷⁰ But he denied it before them all. "I don't know what you're talking about," he said.
>
> ⁷¹ Then he went out to the gateway, where another servant girl saw him and said to the people there, "This fellow was with Jesus of Nazareth."
>
> ⁷² He denied it again, with an oath: "I don't know the man!"
>
> ⁷³ After a little while, those standing there went up to Peter and said, "Surely you are one of them; your accent gives you away."
>
> ⁷⁴ Then he began to call down curses, and he swore to them, "I don't know the man!"
>
> Immediately a rooster crowed. ⁷⁵ Then Peter remembered the word Jesus had spoken: "Before the rooster crows, you will disown me three times." And he went outside and wept bitterly.

Reflecting on God's Word

We've all heard the stories of Peter, Paul, and Judas. We know Peter as the disciple who gave the sermon at Pentecost, walked on water, and denied Jesus three times. Peter was often deemed rash in his judgment, and quick to speak without thinking. He was a bit of a hothead, a know-it-all, one you might think God wouldn't want to use. Similarly, Paul had a less-than-perfect past. He described himself as chief of all sinners, spending much of his life persecuting and killing Christians willfully. Paul, much like Peter, had a complex history, one mired with indiscretions and misguided actions alongside great feats for the cause of Christ. He, too, suffered from bad judgment at pivotal points in his life, but, just as with Peter, God didn't throw him away. God harnessed the good and bad characteristics and transformed both men into powerful examples of being a vessel for God, giving your life to the Lord for his bidding, and allowing the Holy Spirit to fill you with all that is needed to fulfill your God-given mission.

Juxtapose these men with Judas, a man who was a disciple of Jesus. He is described in John 12:4–6 as a thief who had ill intent and a hardened heart, driven by greed and selfishness. As treasurer, the one charged with keeping track of the funds used by the disciples, he often stole money for his selfish pursuits. [1]Although he walked with Jesus daily, the principles and character of Jesus failed to penetrate his heart and mind. He spent much of his energy feeding his flesh, catering to the wants and desires of his heart that there was seemingly no room for the will of God to flourish.

Why do you think Peter and Paul were so successful in pursuing the cause of Christ but not Judas? What do you think sets them apart? Clearly, it's not that they were perfect or didn't make mistakes. If that were the case, we would all be in trouble. I contend that the true distinction between these three men is how they responded when faced with the darkest moment in their lives, the storm that came and knocked the wind out of them, the trial that made them come face to face with God and themselves.

I can only imagine how Peter felt when he realized Jesus' words that he would deny him three times reigned true. When the cock crowed, his heart must have dropped. The guilt and the reality of his sin against Christ were likely unbearable. The scripture says he went away, weeping bitterly. Likewise, with Paul, think about how it must have felt on the way to Damascus. He was bent on finding and killing anyone proclaiming to follow Christ when his mission was thwarted by a voice from Jesus asking, "Why are you persecuting me?" (Acts 9:3). Imagine being faced with the reality that the fervor and zeal you had given to your life-long mission was misdirected. There is a saying that you can spend your whole life climbing a ladder to success, finally making it to the top, only to find that you were on the wrong ladder. What a humbling place to be when you recognize you've been going down the wrong path, drifting further away from God, and you never knew it. Judas, like Paul and Peter, had a day of reckoning—a moment

1. Smith, Verse by Verse Study of John, Ch 12.

when he recognized the damage he had done in betraying Christ. In Matthew 27:3, the scriptures say that "when he realized Jesus had been condemned to die, he was filled with remorse." He even took the money he had been given back to the priests, declaring he had sinned in betraying an innocent man.

All three men were faced with the reality that they had gone against the will of Christ and that there were things in their past they couldn't go back and change no matter how much they wanted to. But how did each respond to this reality? The fact is that all of these men were flawed. They all had problematic characteristics— Peter's rashness and stubborn pride, Paul's passion and dogmatic pursuits, and Judas's greed and selfishness. Just like them, although God may have allowed us to have certain characteristics, we have a choice in how they show up in our lives. The Bible talks about not being a slave to self but bringing ourselves and our thoughts under subjection to the will of Christ (2 Corinthians 10:5). Peter, who wept bitterly over the guilt arising from his denial of Jesus, became a great leader of the faith, preaching to the masses and winning many souls for Christ. Similarly, Paul, once his eyes were opened, got up without hesitation, was baptized, and immediately began preaching that Jesus was the son of God (Acts 9:20). The people were amazed that a man who had imprisoned and killed Christians was now Christ's biggest advocate.

But what became of Judas? Unlike Peter and Paul, he took his guilt, shame, and disappointment and gave in to it. His heart was hardened even more, impermeable to the will of God (John 6:70, John 17:12). If we are not careful, we will also choose self-pity and regret as our path, especially in our storms, giving way to Satan, who wants more than anything for us to focus on ourselves instead of God's unlimited power to work in us. Even Satan knows where our power lies, but we so easily forget. We forget that God can change our circumstances or transform us so that we can endure them, and he is able to shape and mold us into what he wants us to be no matter how soiled we are or how dire the conditions. We forget he is a long-suffering God, not wanting any of us to perish, overflowing with love and compassion for his people.

I wonder, what if Judas had repented, asked for forgiveness for his sin, and decided to turn his life around? What if he had been humble enough to admit his faults and then allow God to transform him and make him over? We'll never know because he chose instead to give up. He chose to believe Satan's lies that there was no overcoming the damage done and no coming back from the pain he caused, so there was no use in trying anymore.

But the reality is we serve a God who is able. With this God, all things are possible. Despite all of the atrocities Paul committed, in Acts 9:15, God says, "Saul is my chosen instrument to take my message to the Gentiles and to kings, as well as to the people of Israel." God sees us in our totality—the good, the bad, the ugly—and if we are willing to turn our lives over to him, he can accomplish miraculous things. God used Paul's fervor and passion and Peter's rash and stubborn nature and directed it toward the cause of Christ, and we and so many other souls have benefited. Are you like Peter and Paul or more like Judas? Whose voice are you heeding in the midst of your storms? I hope you choose the right one.

Questions to Ponder

- Think about a storm you have been through recently. What words describe how you responded in the storm (i.e., self-pity, doubt, prayer, humility)?
- Assess whether your response most resembled Peter, Paul, or Judas?
- Do you think your response was guided by God or Satan? How do you know?
- What are some practical ways you can work to hear and follow God's voice in your storms?

LESSON 7

Sometimes the Lord Takes His Time So He Can Get the Most Glory
The Case of Habakkuk and Daniel

Trusting God's Timing

After four and a half years of marriage, numerous pregnancy tests, and false alarms, we still had no children. I had become wary at the prospect of conceiving, resorting to research on adoption as a viable option. The doctors were starting to get a little concerned. They, like I, figured we would be pregnant by now. I was starting my thirties and was worried that perhaps God just did not have babies in our future. Every time I went for my annual checkup with the doctor, I would get the proverbial "You're not pregnant yet?" as if I was some defective toy or electronic device that could not quite live up to its intended purpose. The doctors and nurses suggested tests to make sure everything was working properly, but I resorted to prayer instead. I did not want to give in to the idea that I could not have children, and I did not want to put my husband through the stress and concern I had endured, so I kept it bottled up and prayed more than ever before. I vowed, like Hannah, that if God blessed me with a child, I would do everything in my power to give them back to him. Still, months went by with no results—until that fateful day.

My husband was away on a boys' trip, and I had not been feeling my best. I decided to take one more pregnancy test and to my surprise, it came back positive. I still did not quite believe it, so I immediately set up an appointment with the doctor to confirm, and by the grace of God, it was finally true. When she came back with the news, I had to contain my emotions—I was so full of joy. But I couldn't help remembering the sleepless nights, the tear-filled pleas to God, and the tightly kept pain I had endured over the last several years. Yet, it was all worth it. I know I would not have appreciated the gift as much if I had not endured the storm. At five years of marriage and thirty-one years of age, we welcomed our first child, and then four and a half years later, our second. The funny thing is we often say we could have waited a little longer to start having kids, but deep down, we know God is always right on time.

What the Bible Says

Daniel's Persistent Prayer

Daniel 10:1–12 NIV

10 In the third year of Cyrus king of Persia, a revelation was given to Daniel (who was called Belteshazzar). Its message was true, and it concerned a great war. The understanding of the message came to him in a vision.

² At that time I, Daniel, mourned for three weeks. ³ I ate no choice food; no meat or wine touched my lips, and I used no lotions at all until the three weeks were over.

⁴ On the twenty-fourth day of the first month, as I was standing on the bank of the great river, the Tigris, ⁵ I looked up and there before me was a man dressed in linen, with a belt of fine gold from Uphaz around his waist. ⁶ His body was like

topaz, his face like lightning, his eyes like flaming torches, his arms and legs like the gleam of burnished bronze, and his voice like the sound of a multitude.

⁷ I, Daniel, was the only one who saw the vision; those who were with me did not see it, but such terror overwhelmed them that they fled and hid themselves. ⁸ So I was left alone, gazing at this great vision; I had no strength left, my face turned deathly pale, and I was helpless. ⁹ Then I heard him speaking, and as I listened to him, I fell into a deep sleep, my face to the ground.

¹⁰ A hand touched me and set me trembling on my hands and knees. ¹¹ He said, "Daniel, you who are highly esteemed, consider carefully the words I am about to speak to you, and stand up, for I have now been sent to you." And when he said this to me, I stood up trembling.

¹² Then he continued, "Do not be afraid, Daniel. Since the first day that you set your mind to gain understanding and to humble yourself before your God, your words were heard, and I have come in response to them."

Habakkuk's Complaint

Habakkuk 1:1–6 NIV

1 The prophecy that Habakkuk the prophet received.

Habakkuk's Complaint

² How long, Lord, must I call for help, but you do not listen? Or cry out to you, "Violence!" but you do not save? ³ Why do you make me look at injustice? Why do you tolerate wrongdoing?

Destruction and violence are before me; there is strife, and conflict abounds. ⁴ Therefore the law is paralyzed, and justice never prevails. The wicked hem in the righteous, so that justice is perverted.

The Lord's Answer

> ⁵ "Look at the nations and watch—and be utterly amazed. For I am going to do something in your days that you would not believe, even if you were told. ⁶ I am raising up the Babylonians, that ruthless and impetuous people, who sweep across the whole earth to seize dwellings not their own . . ."

Reflecting on God's Word

One of the biggest lessons I learned during my storms is that God works in his own perfect timing. God's concept of time does not coincide with our own. We want our storms to be over as quickly as possible, but God may have other plans. I tend to be a bit of a control freak, so I like to make timelines and deadlines and chart out the course of my future. Being placed in a situation in which I have no control is torture. I spent months trying to figure out how to plot my way out of the storm, but eventually, I realized that maybe God just wanted me to sit in it indefinitely. I noticed a cycle with myself and those around me: initial hope you can change things, followed by frustration, anger, and then landing in a state where you give in to the reality that you're unable to fix the situation and that you cannot resolve the problem on your own, throwing up your hands in seeming defeat. I realize now that perhaps that state is exactly where God wants us to be, where we do not have the answers and can't dig ourselves out of the pit we landed in, but we know when we get through the storm, no one but God brought us out. For those with a will like mine, a stubborn resolve to fight until you can't fight anymore, it may take some time until you reach the point where you tap out and accept that your power is inadequate. But, once you come to that acceptance, it opens the door for astounding things to happen.

In Daniel 10:2–3, Daniel undergoes a time when he prayed to God but received no answer. He fasted and prayed, and fasted and prayed some more, with no results. At a certain point, he became so disheartened the Lord decided to send an angel to assure him God had heard his prayer. The angel preceded to tell him that despite hearing his prayer, he faced many hindrances along the way, which delayed his response. He wanted to reassure Daniel that God was watching over him and Israel and working behind the scenes, fighting battles that needed to be fought so that the enemy would not overcome them in the end. Sometimes, unseen forces at work and battles being waged would surely resurface if God did not do everything to extinguish their power over our lives.[1] "For we are not fighting against flesh-and-blood enemies but against evil rulers and authorities of the unseen world, against mighty powers in this dark world, and against evil spirits in the heavenly places." (Ephesians 6:12). We must have faith that God is in control and working things out on our behalf.

Habakkuk, just like Daniel, struggled with God's timing. He asked God how long he must call for help and God not answer (Habakkuk 1:2). He questioned whether God was truly working at all, and he wondered why God allowed evil to persist in the world when he had the power to end it. We tend to do the exact same thing as Habakkuk, particularly in our storms. God is not moving as quickly as we would like, so we assume he is not working at all, but God's response to Habakkuk says it all, "Look around at the nations; look and be amazed! For I am doing something in your own day, something you wouldn't believe even if someone told you about it." (Habakkuk 1:5). Similarly, in Isaiah 43, God promises Israel victory; he says to forget about the past for "it is nothing compared to what I am going to do. For I am about to do something new. See, I have already begun! Do you not see it?" God is working behind the scenes, whether we're aware of it or not, and what he will accomplish is infinitely more than we could ever ask or think (Ephesians 3:20). Perhaps he is trying to do a great work just like he promised to the Israelites in Ezekiel 36:33-36 when he said,

> "On the day I cleanse you from all your sins,
> I will resettle your towns, and the ruins will be rebuilt.
> The desolate land will be cultivated instead of lying desolate
> in the sight of all who pass through it. They will say,
> this land that was laid waste has become like the garden of Eden;

---

1. Guzik, Study Guide for Daniel 10, §4.

> *the cities that were lying in ruins, desolate and destroyed,*
> *are now fortified and inhabited.*
> *Then the nations around you that remain*
> *will know that I the Lord have rebuilt what was destroyed*
> *and have replanted what was desolate."*

Maybe in our storms, God also wants to take our bleak circumstances, wretched behavior, and immeasurable mess and turn it completely around, creating a paradise beyond our wildest imagination. Perhaps, God wants the world and us to know the change that occurs in our circumstances is so grand, so inconceivable to the human mind, that we must recognize it had nothing to do with any effort on our part.

God may allow our storms to continue indefinitely but always for a purpose. Perhaps, there are areas we need to grow spiritually or those around us. Maybe, God wants us to develop a habit of persistent prayer and is busy fighting on our behalf to clear the way toward our victory. But perhaps, God just wants us to acknowledge him as the only one who delivered us, as the one who sustained us and carried us through the storm. Maybe God just wants us to know who really holds the power to save and wants to get all the recognition and honor he is due. In Isaiah 41:20, when God notes he will help Israel, he says, "I am doing this so all who see this miracle will understand what it means—that it is the Lord who has done this . . ." Perhaps, this is why he takes his time, giving us space to do everything in our limited power to endeavor to get ourselves out of our seemingly insurmountable circumstances to no avail. Once we expend all of our energy, tire ourselves out, and no longer have the strength to continue, he can swoop in and remind us of what has been true all along— that this is his battle, he brings the victory, and all of our strength can never compare to the unlimited power that lies in him. Then, we won't have any choice. We won't be able to do anything but give him all the credit, all the glory, and all the praise.

Questions to Ponder

- Think of a time in your life when you prayed to God and received no response. How did that make you feel? How did you react?
- In light of Habakkuk and Daniel's experiences, how could you view your situation differently? How could you have responded in a better way?
- Can you think of other people in the Bible who had similar experiences, having to wait patiently for God to act? What lessons can you take from their experiences to help you when you face similar challenges?

LESSON 8

Make Decisions with the Kingdom in Mind

The Case of Hannah and Sarah

God's Little Blessings

One thing you learn fairly quickly when raising kids is that each one is different. Each has his own personality and tendencies. Year after year, you watch them grow and blossom more fully into whom they will become as an adult. I believe, outside of marriage, child-rearing is one of the hardest tasks to take on. The good thing is it is also one of the most rewarding.

I have had my share of storms while raising kids. All the things I said I would never do, I must admit, I have done more times than I care to voice. I remember, before having kids, seeing other folks' kids act up in public places. I would shake my head in defiance, vowing I would never allow my child to embarrass me like that, but if I had a dollar for the number of times my children humiliated me in Walmart alone, I would be a millionaire by now. The reality is that you never know what you will do in a situation until you are in it, and child-rearing has a way of humbling even the best of us.

Despite the challenges, I made every effort to remain committed to the vow I took years prior when I pleaded with God to bless me with children. From the first few days of their lives, while suffering through postpartum depression, to the woes of toddlerhood and incessant tantrums, I read the Bible and sang hymns with them, which served as a blessing to them and me at the same time. As they got older, we graduated to reading Bible stories every night, conducting Bible studies and devotions at home, and having discussions following Sunday morning sermons to ensure they understood the minister's message. And all of it culminated in one of the best days of my life when they both decided to get baptized in the spring of 2020. There's nothing like hearing your child profess to love God to the point that they want to commit their lives to him. At seven and eleven years of age, they made the wisest decision they would ever make in life. Nothing brings a parent more joy than knowing your little blessings are playing a small part in living out God's purposes here on earth and that your children are truly about the father's business. That day, I felt despite all the mistakes, the struggle to stay sane amid the childhood antics, and the constant belief that I wasn't doing enough, everything leading up to that moment had served a purpose. It all pointed them in the direction of Christ, and I could finally take a moment, take a breath, and recognize that the struggle had all been worth it.

What the Bible Says

Hannah's Faithfulness

1 Samuel 2:1–10 NIV

2 Then Hannah prayed and said:

"My heart rejoices in the LORD; in the LORD my horn is lifted high. My mouth boasts over my enemies, for I delight in your deliverance. ² There is no one holy like the LORD; there is no one besides you; there is no Rock like our God. ³ Do not keep talking so proudly or let your mouth speak such arrogance, for the LORD is a God who knows, and by him deeds are weighed. ⁴ The bows of the warriors are broken, but those who stumbled are armed with strength. ⁵ Those who were full hire themselves out for food, but those who were hungry are hungry no more. She who was barren has borne seven children, but she who has had many sons pines away." ⁶ "The LORD brings death and makes alive; he brings down to the grave and raises up. ⁷ The LORD sends poverty and wealth; he humbles, and he exalts. ⁸ He raises the poor from the dust and lifts the needy from the ash heap; he seats them with princes and has them inherit a throne of honor. For the foundations of the earth are the LORD's; on them he has set the world. ⁹ He will guard the feet of his faithful servants, but the wicked will be silenced in the place of darkness. It is not by strength that one prevails; ¹⁰ those who oppose the LORD will be broken. The Most High will thunder from heaven; the LORD will judge the ends of the earth. He will give strength to his king and exalt the horn of his anointed."

Sarah's Folly

Genesis 16:1–6 NIV

16 Now Sarai, Abram's wife, had borne him no children. But she had an Egyptian slave named Hagar; ² so she said to Abram, "The LORD has kept me from having children. Go, sleep with my slave; perhaps I can build a family through her."

Abram agreed to what Sarai said. ³ So after Abram had been living in Canaan ten years, Sarai his wife took her Egyptian slave Hagar and gave her to her husband to be his wife. ⁴ He slept with Hagar, and she conceived.

When she knew she was pregnant, she began to despise her mistress. ⁵ Then Sarai said to Abram, "You are responsible for the wrong I am suffering. I put my slave in your arms, and

> now that she knows she is pregnant, she despises me. May the LORD judge between you and me."
>
> ⁶ "Your slave is in your hands," Abram said. "Do with her whatever you think best." Then Sarai mistreated Hagar; so, she fled from her.

Reflecting on God's Word

We all know the story of Hannah, a woman who was barren and prayed mightily to God for a child. She made a vow that if God gave her a child, she would make sure he was returned to him. Hannah, in her need, was thinking about the Kingdom. She was concerned about bringing glory and honor to God through her offspring. How many of us think about how the things we desire can bring glory to God? How often do we consider, when we're making decisions, if our choice is the one that brings him the most glory? This is particularly important in our storms. Storms are an especially opportune way for God to shape us and mold us into who he wants us to be, but how often do we pray for God to get us out of the storm, not at all concerned with what God may be trying to produce in us to bring glory to the Kingdom?

Instead of being like Hannah, many of us more closely resemble Sarah. Sarah was a woman with a similar problem as Hannah—she too was barren. Whereas Hannah prayed to God to address her issue, Sarah took matters into her own hands, offering her maid to her husband. Instead of consulting God, she concocted her own plan, which would come back to haunt her, as most of our ill-gotten plans do. She did not have the Kingdom in mind when she made her plans; she only wanted to ensure she accomplished her goal at all costs. How often do we do the same, going about life making decisions that run contrary to God's will because we are more concerned about our desires instead of the betterment of the Kingdom? We are more concerned about our will being done instead of considering what God's plans for our lives may be. We spend so much time trying to live out our own truth that we never consider that God's truth about us and who he intends us to be is really all that matters. Finding your truth and having it not align with God's will for your life is for naught. Also, finding your truth and it not benefiting the Kingdom is futile for anyone professing to be a child of God.

Woe to us all if we are left to our own devices to determine the plans for our life. We are surely hopeless if we relegate God's working in our lives to our own finite wisdom. God can do far more than we could ever imagine (Ephesians 3:20), even bring manna from heaven (Exodus 16:4), part the Red Sea (Exodus 14:21), bring water from a rock (Exodus 17:1–7), feed five thousand with five loaves of bread and two fish (Matthew 14:13–21), and calm all kinds of storms (Matthew 8:26). God can bring a blessing from the unlikeliest of places. God can even take what Satan meant for evil and use it for his glory.

This journey we are on is bigger than you and I. God and his purposes must be at the core of everything we do, and our lives should reflect this reality. The fact is that either our actions lead to the betterment of the Kingdom or its worsening. It's either one or the other; there is no gray area in between. Joshua proclaims in Joshua 24:15, "choose for yourselves this day who you will serve but as for me and my house, we will serve the Lord." God is counting on us to choose a life that is pleasing to him, to love him, and care enough about our own salvation and the salvation of those around us to live righteously, keeping the Kingdom at the forefront of our minds. Our children and the generations that follow are depending on us to keep the faith, so let us valiantly carry the torch, passing it graciously on to the next in line to continue the legacy of a strong and everlasting commitment to running the Christian race and furthering the goals of the Kingdom.

Questions to Ponder

- ❂ Think of a major life decision you have made (i.e., marriage, college, etc.). Before you made the decision, did you consider how it would further or hinder the Kingdom of God?

- Looking back now, would you have made the same decision if you had the Kingdom in mind? Why or why not?
- What are some practical ways you can be intentional about considering the will of God before you make life decisions?

LESSON 9

You Can't Choose Which of God's Commands to Follow

The Case of Jesus and the Prodigal Son

Workplace Woes

Difficult people can put a damper on our lives at times. From the start of my career, I have had to navigate some personalities that presented challenges to my faith. One of the most harrowing experiences is having to walk into an office every day and submit to the will of a person you know does not always have your best interest at heart. People who have their own motivations and, ultimately, put their interests at the forefront can make life miserable for you if you let them.

I have had my share of bosses who would fit this category, and for the most part, I have been able to get along with everyone, but one proved to be a storm that tested my faith in ways I could not believe. I am a pretty independent person and pride myself on not needing a lot of direction. Just give me a task and leave it to me to get it done. But some people want to put their finger on everything and constantly look over your shoulder to make sure you are doing what you should, and one boss took micromanagement to the next level.

I found myself butting heads with her incessantly. She was a storm that landed unexpectedly and wreaked havoc on everything in its territory. Within months of her arrival, half of the staff on my team left for other jobs, and numerous others filed complaints against her. In her short two-year span in our office, she effectively turned everyone against her, and to be honest, even me. I had to pray mightily every day for the strength to deal with her and not compromise my faith. Before I knew it, I found my always quiet, meek persona transformed into the person challenging her in meetings. I felt the need to assure her I could handle the tasks set before me, and after a couple of dueling matches and uncomfortable exchanges, she started to get the message.

One day, the Holy Spirit showed me the impetus behind her misconduct. As a team-building activity, we all were asked to complete a personality test. In our debriefing session, we had to assess why we think we respond in situations the way we do. In a moment of transparency, she shared information about her childhood and the constant feeling of never living up to her mother's expectations. "Nothing was ever enough," she said. It became clear that to feel secure in her own ability, she often acted out in ways that bolstered her own image and minimized everyone else's. In many ways, she had become her mother, and this exhibited itself in lording over others to prove to herself and those around her that she was capable.

We rarely think about why people act the way they do, and relationships often suffer because of it. Making it clear to her that I could handle the assignments given to me by following through successfully over time and assuring her I would stand up to her or anyone else to defend my work ethic and ability provided her the parameters she needed to let go. And today, we are on good terms. Even though she is no longer my boss, she still reaches out if she needs a favor or needs help with a task and wants to have total confidence in the one handling it.

Today, I am grateful that God allowed me to maintain peace in our relationship, and I wish I could take credit for the outcome, but I know if left to my own devices, things would have fared quite differently. I watched others who left the team burn bridges that may never be mended, and the truth is, you never know when you will have to come face to face with people again. Now, I am grateful that I heeded the Holy Spirit and chose to move past our differences and see her as a person of value despite her insecurities and the inappropriate way they may have shown up. The world may see my approach as a weakness, showing compassion and tolerance despite how people treat you, but it takes incredible strength and humility to face such challenges head-on in this way. Dealing with difficult people may remain a challenge, but we are not absolved of the responsibility to love and respect them despite how they treat us. God's commands, no matter how difficult, are still binding.

What the Bible Says

A Father's Restoring Spirit

Luke 15:11–32 NIV

[11] Jesus continued: "There was a man who had two sons. [12] The younger one said to his father, 'Father, give me my share of the estate.' So, he divided his property between them. [13] Not long after that, the younger son got together all he had, set off for a distant country and there squandered his wealth in wild living. [14] After he had spent everything, there was a severe famine in that whole country, and he began to be in need. [15] So he went and hired himself out to a citizen of that country, who sent him to his fields to feed pigs. [16] He longed to fill his stomach with the pods that the pigs were eating, but no one gave him anything.

[17] When he came to his senses, he said, 'How many of my father's hired servants have food to spare, and here I am starving to death! [18] I will set out and go back to my father and say to him: Father, I have sinned against heaven and against you. [19] I am no longer worthy to be called your son; make me like one

of your hired servants.' ²⁰ So he got up and went to his father. But while he was still a long way off, his father saw him and was filled with compassion for him; he ran to his son, threw his arms around him and kissed him. ²¹ The son said to him, 'Father, I have sinned against heaven and against you. I am no longer worthy to be called your son.'²² But the father said to his servants, 'Quick! Bring the best robe and put it on him. Put a ring on his finger and sandals on his feet. ²³ Bring the fattened calf and kill it. Let's have a feast and celebrate. ²⁴ For this son of mine was dead and is alive again; he was lost and is found.' So, they began to celebrate.

²⁵ Meanwhile, the older son was in the field. When he came near the house, he heard music and dancing. ²⁶ So he called one of the servants and asked him what was going on. ²⁷ 'Your brother has come,' he replied, 'and your father has killed the fattened calf because he has him back safe and sound.'²⁸ The older brother became angry and refused to go in. So, his father went out and pleaded with him. ²⁹ But he answered his father, 'Look! All these years I've been slaving for you and never disobeyed your orders. Yet you never gave me even a young goat so I could celebrate with my friends. ³⁰ But when this son of yours who has squandered your property with prostitutes comes home, you kill the fattened calf for him!'³¹ 'My son,' the father said, 'you are always with me, and everything I have is yours. ³² But we had to celebrate and be glad, because this brother of yours was dead and is alive again; he was lost and is found.'"

Jesus' Righteous Command

John 13:1–15 NIV

13 It was just before the Passover Festival. Jesus knew that the hour had come for him to leave this world and go to the Father. Having loved his own who were in the world, he loved them to the end.

² The evening meal was in progress, and the devil had already prompted Judas, the son of Simon Iscariot, to betray Jesus. ³ Jesus knew that the Father had put all things under his power, and that he had come from God and was returning to God; ⁴ so he got up from the meal, took off his outer clothing, and wrapped a towel around his waist. ⁵ After that, he poured water into a basin and began to wash his disciples' feet, drying them with the towel that was wrapped around him.

⁶ He came to Simon Peter, who said to him, "Lord, are you going to wash my feet?"

⁷ Jesus replied, "You do not realize now what I am doing, but later you will understand."

⁸ "No," said Peter, "you shall never wash my feet."

Jesus answered, "Unless I wash you, you have no part with me."

⁹ "Then, Lord," Simon Peter replied, "not just my feet but my hands and my head as well!"

¹⁰ Jesus answered, "Those who have had a bath need only to wash their feet; their whole body is clean. And you are clean, though not every one of you." ¹¹ For he knew who was going to betray him, and that was why he said not everyone was clean.

¹² When he had finished washing their feet, he put on his clothes and returned to his place. "Do you understand what I have done for you?" he asked them. ¹³ "You call me 'Teacher' and 'Lord,' and rightly so, for that is what I am. ¹⁴ Now that I, your Lord and Teacher, have washed your feet, you also should wash one another's feet. ¹⁵ I have set you an example that you should do as I have done for you."

Reflecting on God's Word

When we are in our storms, at first glance, some of the things God asks of us may seem unreasonable. There may be instances where God asks us to forgive someone who hurt us, mistreated us, or wronged us somehow. In the storm, God may ask us to stand still and not fight but wait on him to fight our battles for us. Oftentimes, the things God requests of us seem impossible to do, and truthfully, perhaps they are when working with our own limited might. Luckily, God has given us access to the power of the Holy Spirit to make seemingly impossible tasks more manageable.

The parable in Luke 15:11–32 about the prodigal son always troubled me when I was younger, and it was not until I was in the middle of one of my worst storms that I was able to conceptualize the breadth and depth of its meaning. I had always viewed this story from the standpoint of the older son, who never left. I had always looked at the lost son in contempt, questioning why the father had welcomed him back with open arms. I realize now my self-righteousness wouldn't allow me to fully appreciate the majesty of the father's love, and thus, God's love. My view of God was deficient, hindering me from fully recognizing the true magnitude of his grace and mercy. I had spent my life telling myself and others that I believed in God's grace and ability to save everyone, but in reality, I had relegated his love and salvation to those who met my standard and were as right as I was in my own imperfect eyes. Today, I recognize my sin as no less than anyone else's and that it is subject to the same mercy and grace as any other. I, too, am in the same proverbial boat as those with the *greatest* of sins that cannot be hidden and defended when held up against the word of God. No one who believes in the authority of the Bible would argue, even the perpetrator himself, that murder or fornication are not a violation of God's tenets, but there are many other sins committed every second under the veil of silence that are only known to the person committing them and God. I realize now they are all the same in God's perfect eyes.

Praise Him Anyway: The Blessing Is the Storm

In one of my storms, I was reckoned with the command to forgive in ways I had never before. Like the father in Luke 15, I had been offended and had every right to be angry, resentful, and to even seek atonement for the wrongs done. But, when faced with this reality, I recognized that the father swallowed his shame and sought to make amends even though he had every right to the alternative. He had every right to be furious, hold a grudge, and even disown his son, but, instead, he put aside his pride and chose forgiveness and restoration.[1] In my storm, I was faced with similar feelings of anger and hurt, and my response surprised me as well as those around me. When asked why I did not seem to give in to the hurt and anger in the way others often did in my situation, my response was, "I have felt all of those emotions, but I choose not to stay there." I knew, from past experiences, where those emotions led. They were a straight and certain path to resentment and bitterness. Those emotions moved you to do things you never thought you would do and become who you never thought you would become. I knew the destination well because I had been there before, but now I knew once and for all that was not where God wanted me to reside. He wanted a life far greater for me.

Today, I recognize that God calls us to a form of forgiveness that this world cannot even begin to comprehend. It is outside the bounds of this world's definition or interpretation. He calls us not only to forgive but to seek, whenever possible, reconciliation and restoration. The father personified the love of Christ, exemplifying true forgiveness and grace by restoring the lost son to his prior position. He chose to see his son as someone of value even though he did not deserve such treatment. Restoration showed he had truly forgiven, had put aside the wrong done, and was willing to put the past behind him and move forward into the new. Isaiah 43 speaks to the act of putting the past behind and embracing the new thing God is trying to accomplish. What a difficult task to take on, but the challenge and the struggle required do not make it any less of an obligation to God.

---

1. Spurgeon, "Many Kisses for Returning Sinners", para. 6–9.

You Can't Choose Which of God's Commands to Follow

This concept is further illustrated when Jesus showcases what it means to be a servant when he washes the disciples' feet. He humbled himself, serving those who would deny him and even betray him days later. The beauty and miracle in this account are he washed their feet, knowing the harm they were about to inflict on him and the extent to which their actions would plague him in the end.[2] Most of us do not have that level of compassion to pardon someone's sin against us before they even repent or ask for forgiveness. In Matthew 18:21–22, when Peter asked, "Lord, how oft should my brother sin against me, and I forgive him?" Jesus told him to forgive his brother who sinned against him seventy times seven. This speaks to the level at which God calls us to forgive those who malign us, exonerate those who betray our trust and absolve those who selfishly misuse us with no regard for the suffering they cause.

Living out the principle of forgiveness exemplified in these accounts seemed inconceivable in my youth, but I know now everything in God's word is indisputable, and everything is possible with the working of the Holy Spirit in us. Second Timothy 3:16–17 asserts that "all scripture is inspired by God and is useful to teach us what is true and to make us realize what is wrong in our lives . . . God uses it to prepare and equip his people to do every good work." Thus, his word is for our edification and is ultimately for our learning and spiritual development. We cannot choose which scriptures we wish to follow, no matter how difficult the command may seem. God often asks us to go the extra mile and go above and beyond—not to operate by the world's standards but to exhibit God's standards for living. God ultimately wants us to follow his lead. In Genesis 22:2, Abraham is commanded to do the unthinkable. He is called to kill the son he had prayed so many years for and sacrifice him at God's behest. Abraham was called to obey God's command and trust him to take care of the outcome. And we are called to do the same. Are you up for the challenge, or will you retreat under the auspices that it is too difficult? God's commands are immutable, and it is incumbent upon us as Jesus'

2. Guzik, Study Guide for John 13, §A3.

followers to heed not only the commands we deem reasonable but those only possible through the help of the Holy Spirit working mightily through us.

Questions to Ponder

- ❂ Think about a command in the Bible you think would be difficult for you to follow. Meditate on scriptures pertaining to that command and come up with practical ways you can work on following that command during the coming week.
- ❂ Pray that the Holy Spirit helps you as you endeavor to complete this task. Take note of ways you notice the Holy Spirit at work in you during the week.
- ❂ In what ways did the enemy try to get you not to follow through on completing this task? Based on the enemy's tactics, what are some practical ways you can resist him in the future?

LESSON 10

God Does Not Owe You an Explanation

The Case of Job and Paul

Seeking Fulfillment

After starting my career in the summer of 2004, I quickly realized my job was not as fulfilling as I had hoped it would be. After sailing through undergrad and graduate school, I thought, surely, I would embark on the job of my life, one where I could change the world and make it a better place, where I could fulfill dreams I'd had since I was a child. But one year in, I could not deny that the job I had put so much stock in did not quite measure up to the dream. I even started mentioning to my husband, to his dismay, that, "I'd like to start over and go to art school." I was disillusioned and felt all the hard work I put in and all the effort I thought would pay off had not been worth it. My husband encouraged me to stay positive and push through, but deep down, I held onto the belief that there was something more God had in store; he just had yet to reveal it.

Disillusionment or disappointment can be some of the worst storms we encounter. These feelings can overtake us if not properly managed and make us question everything God has already and continues to accomplish in our lives. This is pointed out in the landmark film, "*It's a Wonderful Life,*" where God is speaking with the angel about the plight of the main character, George. God says, "George is in trouble," and the angel responds, "What's wrong with him? Is he sick?" God's response is, "No. Worse. He's discouraged." Those who have seen the movie know that George was considering suicide because of money problems he encountered. What a powerful testament to the tremendous detriment disappointment and disillusionment can cause in our lives. By the end of the movie, George, faced with the possibility of losing everything he had, realized he actually had a wonderful life—he just had to open his eyes and see it.

Although I may not have gone to the extreme that George did when faced with disappointments in my career, I have to admit in my periods of disillusionment, there were times I felt like giving up, but I thank God that he sustained my faith during these weakest moments. In my discouragement, instead of giving up, he led me to press on and seek opportunities that piqued my interest at work. I was allowed to carve out time to complete extra work that provided the fulfillment I sought. The long hours spent after work drafting manuscripts and publishing articles, the internships and detail opportunities I pursued, and the additional training and workshops to augment my work provided the outlet I needed to find purpose in my efforts. During those years, there were times I lamented having to work so hard when it seemed that those around me had it easy, and I questioned why God would not send me that "perfect" job where I could fuse my passion, experience, and training. But although I prayed for years to God for an explanation, he did not answer.

In the interim, I pursued creative outlets such as writing, drawing, painting, and photography while continuing to progress in my career. Despite the efforts of my employers, I passed on leadership position after leadership position that people offered me because I knew God had a different calling for me, even if I did not know quite yet what it was. And years later, when the storm of my life hit, God finally lifted the veil. He gave me permission to lean into the storm, take advantage of the enlightenment that only

God Does Not Owe You an Explanation

comes through suffering, and push forward despite not knowing where I would land. I had faced so much disappointment until then and had encountered so much turmoil in the storm that the sting of further discontent no longer stifled me. Fear no longer had the power over me that it had before. My purpose became clearer, and before I knew it, that purpose became greater than any fears I faced. I published my first book during the storm and started working on a second one. I also landed my dream job, one that finally made all of my experiences thus far on my career path make sense.

After years of not hearing an explanation from God, I relinquished the will to know what God had in store for my career and made the most of the opportunities he provided right in front of me. I maintain that often that is all he asks of us, to not seek fulfillment in the things we think we need but do not yet have, but to find contentment in him and his provision right now. As it's often said, "You have to bloom where you're planted." (Bishop of Geneva St. Francis de Sales). Philippians 4:11–12 further exemplifies this sentiment, ". . . I have learned to be content whatever the circumstances. I know what it is to be in need, and I know what it is to have plenty. I have learned the secret of being content in any and every situation, whether well fed or hungry, whether living in plenty or in want." The work, effort, long hours, and sacrifices paid off, and all of the experiences leading up to the present made me appreciate the blessings all the more. Perhaps God held off on fulfilling my dreams earlier because he knew I was not prepared, or he knew I would take them for granted and not recognize fully God's grace at work. Maybe he held off because he knew at the lowest point of my life, I would need to see his hand at work in ways I had prayed for so many years. Either way, God doesn't always explain the why, especially when we are going through challenging circumstances. But we still must trust the process, knowing it will all make sense in the end.

What the Bible Says

Job's Blessed Epiphany

Job 42:1–6 NIV

42 Then Job replied to the Lord:

² "I know that you can do all things; no purpose of yours can be thwarted. ³ You asked, 'Who is this that obscures my plans without knowledge?' Surely, I spoke of things I did not understand, things too wonderful for me to know. ⁴ You said, 'Listen now, and I will speak; I will question you, and you shall answer me.' ⁵ My ears had heard of you but now my eyes have seen you. ⁶ Therefore I despise myself and repent in dust and ashes."

Reflecting on God's Word

One August morning, I woke up at 6:00 a.m. to watch the sunrise on Kure Beach in North Carolina. It was a humbling experience to watch the sun peek from the depths of the earth, ushering itself forth from behind the morning haze, bringing forth the beauty and majesty that can only come from God. What a perspective to have when going through life's storms, to know that a new dawn is on the horizon every morning, bringing with it a host of possibilities and new beginnings. As the sun made its way into the sky, God's light showed across the water, reflecting the goodness of his glory. And so, it is with our lives. From the bleakness of night and the darkness of our struggles comes the constant reminder that daybreak will eventually come, and its magnificence will be so great that its awesome power cannot be denied. Its shining light is so bright that our hearts and minds will not be able to contain it all. We should all live out the words in the scripture, "This is the day the Lord has made. Let us rejoice and be glad in it." (Psalms 118:24). Knowing our creator ushers in a new day every morning should make us more willing to "commit everything we do to the Lord... and to trust him..." (Psalms 37:5-6).

In my storms, I learned many lessons, but perhaps, the greatest one was that God does not owe me any explanation. I learned a lesson that Job learned during his difficult trials. Job was a man who lost just about everything: his livelihood, family, and health; yet he still refused to curse God. Job's steadfast commitment to God is admirable and, to many of us, seemingly unattainable. But we often forget that amid his steadfast faith, he questioned God about why he had brought him into the world and why bad things were happening to him even though he had done his best to follow God's commands. However, although he asked many questions, Job never learned what was happening behind the scenes, he never learned of the conversations between God and Satan, and he never came to know the overall purpose behind his suffering. He spent a lot of time and energy, just as we do, trying to answer many questions to figure out God's plans, attempting to understand God's thinking and assess God's timing. I imagine he spent countless hours wondering if God was still working on his behalf and if he was still truly by his side through it all. His incessant pleas to God are an example to us that God wants us to pour our hearts out to him also. He wants us to feel so close to him that we are comfortable expressing our pain, discomfort, and joys. Despite Job's pleas, he never got the answers he was looking for, and often we, too, never learn why we are going through the storms of life that beset us.

Although Job's situation seemed dreary, it is evidence that God can test us with one hand and support us with the other. The reality is that although Job felt alone, God was right beside him the whole time, just like he was with Jonah, Hannah, Joseph, Peter, Paul, and others we have mentioned previously. His presence is evidenced by the fact that God only allowed Job to suffer for a finite time, he restricted what Satan could do to him, he sustained his life, and he used Satan as a tool to accomplish his ultimate purpose, which was to make Job a man of even greater faith. How wonderful it is to know that God can do it all. He can try our faith and sustain it all at once, take what Satan meant for evil and make it benefit us in the end, and tear us down and build us up even stronger than before.

At the beginning of the book of Job, he is described as a "blameless man, a man of complete integrity . . . one who feared God and stayed away from evil." (Job 1:1). By the end of the book, Job says to the Lord, "I had only heard about you before, but now I have seen you with my own eyes." (Job 42:5). It is one thing to know about God or believe in him, but the real test is if we trust him. Job's statement teaches us that there is only so far you can go just hearing about God—learning about him through the scriptures, hearing sermons about him on Sunday morning, or testimonies from others about his goodness. There is something life-changing about *experiencing* God, feeling his presence, seeing his hand move in your life, and seeing the awe and grandeur of God in true form.[1] The truth is that oftentimes the only time we come face to face with God is during our darkest moments, our storms. These are the times when we lean on him the most. Job had to lose it all to face the reality of who God really was—sovereign, all-knowing, and all-powerful. Just like Job, we, too, must go through storms in our lives to recognize the majesty of God. We must come to a point where we recognize we do not have all the answers, that God's ways and plans are far better than our own, and that God's wisdom and mercy are more than sufficient. We must see ourselves for what we really are in our weakness and ignorance and juxtapose it with who God is in his infinite wisdom. We must come to the point where we bow before God and make the statement, ". . . you asked, who is this that questions my wisdom with such ignorance? It is I and I was talking about things I knew nothing about, things far too wonderful for me." (Job 42:3). Perhaps, your storm is God testing your faith like Job, or perhaps, it's God's punishment like Jonah, but whatever it is, we must trust that God knows what he is doing, recognize that God is sovereign, and acknowledge that he doesn't owe us some grand explanation—he just is.

---

1. Guzik, Study Guide for Job 42, §A2.

In my storms, I learned so many lessons that have helped enhance my faith. It became apparent, just like with Job, that I had no right to question the goodness of God, no matter how much pain and suffering I experienced. The one who created the universe is all-powerful, all-knowing, and able to work all things together for my good. He doesn't need my help nor does he require my assistance to accomplish his will. It became clear that he is God all by himself, and I have to trust him without wavering.

Perhaps, the greatest lesson we can all learn is that not only are there blessings in the storm, but maybe the blessing *is* the storm. The storm may be the only divine mechanism God uses to bring us closer to him, get us back in alignment with his will, and help us see his miraculous power at work in and around us. Without the storm, I shudder to think who I would be, for it is in the storm that I came face to face with God, came to know and trust him, and truly believe in his power. May we all follow Paul's example when he spoke of suffering the loss of all things to gain Christ (Philippians 3:8). May we use our storms as a means to "know him and the power of His resurrection, and the fellowship of His sufferings . . ." (Philippians 3:10). I pray that we see our storms as our saving grace, put our storms to good use, and do not see them only as situations we run from or beg God to get us out of as quickly as possible. I pray we can say, "My suffering was good for me, for it taught me to pay attention to your decrees." (Psalm 119:71). I pray that we are open and humble enough to know God is right there in the midst, and he will not let our storms overtake us as long as we trust in him to do a great work for us and within us.

Questions to Ponder

- ❁ What are the greatest lessons you have learned in your storms? How can you use those lessons to help you and others in future storms?

Praise Him Anyway: The Blessing Is the Storm

✵ Looking back over your life, can you think of storms you have experienced that you now thank the Lord for bringing your way?

✵ Meditate on Jeremiah 17:7–8. What does this scripture tell us about how we should operate in life's storms? List some other key scriptures that bring you comfort and peace in the midst of your storms.

> [7] "... blessed is the one who trusts in the Lord,
> whose confidence is in him.
> [8] They will be like a tree planted by the water
> that sends out its roots by the stream.
> It does not fear when heat comes;
> its leaves are always green.
> It has no worries in a year of drought
> and never fails to bear fruit."
> Jeremiah 17:7–8 NIV

Afterword

February 3, 2022, proved to be one of the rainiest days of the year. It rained nonstop all day long, culminating in dangerous thunderstorms and torrential downpours that night. This day also happened to be my birthday. Although I was still very much in the midst of my latest storm, when I woke up that fateful morning, things felt different. There was a strange calm I had not felt over the last several months; a peace had taken over. I woke up and immediately prayed like I do every morning, but this prayer was laced with nothing but gratitude. Every other morning, I would start off honoring God for who he is and what he has done but quickly segue into my prayer for relief from the current problem of the day. But this morning, my problems never even rose to the surface of my consciousness. I thanked God for allowing me to see another year and prayed for the strength and resolve to accept the opportunities he had in store for me.

That spirit of gratitude continued as my kids surprised me at 6:45 a.m. with the "Happy Birthday" song and a gift they had cunningly crafted on their own without my knowledge. It continued as I visited the spa for a day of pampering and as my husband surprised me with an unexpected gift later that day. It also continued as we drove through the storm to make our dinner reservations, and my daughter looked at the clouds and said, "It looks like a tornado is coming." I smiled because I was on cloud nine, even with the thunder, rain, and clouds surrounding me. It didn't matter if a tornado was around the corner. I was not going to let anything, not even the weather, damper this perfect day. I kept pressing through despite the ominous look of things.

This day became a testimony to the power of God working in my life throughout my storms. In a conversation with my girlfriend the day before, she was amazed that despite the storm I had been going through, God had blessed me to still be thriving in the middle of it, as evidenced by my finishing the first draft of this book. Sometimes, we talk about surviving our storms or being in the midst of a storm, but as my minister notes, it is important that we are not just in a storm but that we are moving through it and are not in a stagnant state, where growth and development are not occurring. This book is perhaps a witness to God moving me through the storm, showcasing the lessons that I have learned along the way and continue to learn to this day. And although the storm has not moved, I am certain I have. I am not the person I was when my storm began, and though I still have my bad days, I try my best not to cower beneath their weight. I don't always succeed, but I assert that all God asks of us is that we power through, don't give up, and press toward the mark (Philippians 3:13–14). He knows we will falter and stumble, but he will never let us fall because he is holding us by the hand and ordering our steps (Psalms 37:24).

I have to admit I had hoped I would be out of this storm by now, but I realize that God has a purpose for every storm we face, and the storms will remain until they accomplish the goals for which they were intended. Perhaps, my prayer should evolve from asking God to remove the storm or even asking him to help me endure the storm to, *Lord, I pray that the purpose you want to accomplish through the storm is fulfilled.* I pray this book will challenge us all to change our perspective, to see our storms differently, and even appreciate them for the great work they can accomplish in each of us. James 1:2–5 says, "Consider it pure joy, my brothers and sisters, whenever you face trials of many kinds because you know that the testing of your faith produces perseverance. Let perseverance finish its work so that you may be mature and complete, not lacking anything." I pray that we let our storms do what they are designed to do, to ultimately move us closer to God and his purpose for our lives.

Afterword

[8] "*We are hard pressed on every side, but not crushed; perplexed, but not in despair;* [9] *persecuted, but not abandoned; struck down, but not destroyed.* [10] *We always carry around in our body the death of Jesus, so that the life of Jesus may also be revealed in our body.* [11] *For we who are alive are always being given over to death for Jesus' sake, so that his life may also be revealed in our mortal body.* [12] *So then, death is at work in us, but life is at work in you.*

[13] *It is written: 'I believed; therefore, I have spoken.' Since we have that same spirit of faith, we also believe and therefore speak,* [14] *because we know that the one who raised the Lord Jesus from the dead will also raise us with Jesus and present us with you to himself.* [15] *All this is for your benefit, so that the grace that is reaching more and more people may cause thanksgiving to overflow to the glory of God.*

[16] *Therefore we do not lose heart. Though outwardly we are wasting away, yet inwardly we are being renewed day by day.* [17] *For our light and momentary troubles are achieving for us an eternal glory that far outweighs them all.* [18] *So we fix our eyes not on what is seen, but on what is unseen, since what is seen is temporary, but what is unseen is eternal.*" 2 Corinthians 4:8–18 NIV

AMEN

Bibliography

Guzik, David. "Study Guide for 2 Corinthians 4 by David Guzik." Blue Letter Bible. Last Modified 21 Feb,2017. https://www.blueletterbible.org/Comm/guzik_david/StudyGuide2017-2Cr/2Cr-4.cfm

———. "Study Guide for Daniel 10 by David Guzik." Blue Letter Bible. Last Modified 21 Feb,2017. https://www.blueletterbible.org/Comm/guzik_david/StudyGuide2017-Dan/Dan-10.cfm

———. "Study Guide for Isaiah 49 by David Guzik." Blue Letter Bible. Last Modified 21 Feb, 2017. https://www.blueletterbible.org/Comm/guzik_david/StudyGuide2017-Isa/Isa-49.cfm

———. "Study Guide for Job 42 by David Guzik." Blue Letter Bible. Last Modified 21 Feb,2017. https://www.blueletterbible.org/Comm/guzik_david/StudyGuide2017-Job/Job-42.cfm

———. "Study Guide for John 13 by David Guzik." Blue Letter Bible. Last Modified 21 Feb,2017. https://www.blueletterbible.org/Comm/guzik_david/StudyGuide2017-Jhn/Jhn-13.cfm

———. "Study Guide for Luke 8 by David Guzik." Blue Letter Bible. Last Modified 21 Feb,2017. https://www.blueletterbible.org/Comm/guzik_david/StudyGuide2017-Luk/Luk-8.cfm

———. "Study Guide for Numbers 22 by David Guzik." Blue Letter Bible. Last Modified 21 Feb,2017. https://www.blueletterbible.org/Comm/guzik_david/StudyGuide2017-Num/Num-22.cfm

———. "Study Guide for Psalm 23 by David Guzik." Blue Letter Bible. Last Modified 21 Feb,2017. https://www.blueletterbible.org/Comm/guzik_david/StudyGuide2017-Psa/Psa-23.cfm

———. "Study Guide for 2 Thessalonians 2 by David Guzik." Blue Letter Bible. Last Modified 21 Feb,2017. https://www.blueletterbible.org/Comm/guzik_david/StudyGuide2017-2Th/2Th-2.cfm

Henry, Matthew. "Commentary on Jonah 1 by Matthew Henry." Blue Letter Bible. Last Modified 1 Mar,1996. https://www.blueletterbible.org/Comm/mhc/Jon/Jon_001.cfm

———. "Commentary on Mark 4 by Matthew Henry." Blue Letter Bible. Last Modified 1 Mar,1996. https://www.blueletterbible.org/Comm/mhc/Mar/Mar_004.cfm

Bibliography

Jamieson, Robert, et al. "Commentary on Numbers 22 by Jamieson, Fausset & Brown." Blue Letter Bible. Last Modified 19 Feb,2000. https://www.blueletterbible.org/Comm/jfb/Num/Num_022.cfm

Newton, Glenn. "The Heart of Unrealized Potential." In *God Looks at the Heart: A Study of First Samuel*, 35–40. Nashville, TN: 21st Century Christian, 2014.

Plagens, Julie. "Why Jesus Compares Us to Sheep (It's Kinda Funny)." *Christian Parenting*. (October 2020). https://www.christianparenting.org/articles/why-jesus-compares-us-to-sheep-its-kinda-funny/

Smith, Chuck. "Sermon Notes for Mark 4:40 by Chuck Smith." Blue Letter Bible. Last Modified 1 May,2005. https://www.blueletterbible.org/Comm/smith_chuck/SermonNotes_Mar/Mar_15.cfm

———. "Verse by Verse Study on Ezekiel 36–39 (C2000) by Chuck Smith." Blue Letter Bible. Last Modified 1 Jun,2005. https://www.blueletterbible.org/Comm/smith_chuck/c2000_Eze/Eze_036.cfm

———. "Verse by Verse Study on John 11–12 (C2000) by Chuck Smith." Blue Letter Bible. Last Modified 1 Jun,2005. https://www.blueletterbible.org/Comm/smith_chuck/c2000_Jhn/Jhn_011.cfm

Spurgeon, C.H. "Many Kisses for Returning Sinners, Or Prodigal Love for the Prodigal Son by C. H. Spurgeon." Blue Letter Bible. Last Modified 18 Apr, 2001. https://www.blueletterbible.org/Comm/spurgeon_charles/sermons/2236.cfm

www.ingramcontent.com/pod-product-compliance
Lightning Source LLC
Chambersburg PA
CBHW070321100426
42743CB00011B/2507